Getting Started with Windows 8 Apps

Ben Dewey

O'REILLY®

Beijing · Cambridge · Farnham · Köln · Sebastopol · Tokyo

Getting Started with Windows 8 Apps

by Ben Dewey

Published by O'Reilly Media, Inc., 1005 Gravenstein Highway North, Sebastopol, CA 95472.

O'Reilly books may be purchased for educational, business, or sales promotional use. Online editions are also available for most titles (*http://my.safaribooksonline.com*). For more information, contact our corporate/institutional sales department: 800-998-9938 or *corporate@oreilly.com*.

Editor:	Rachel Roumeliotis	**Cover Designer:**	Karen Montgomery
Production Editor:	Melanie Yarbrough	**Interior Designer:**	David Futato
Proofreader:	Melanie Yarbrough	**Illustrator:**	Robert Romano

Revision History for the First Edition:

2012-07-23	First release
2012-08-10	Second release

See *http://oreilly.com/catalog/errata.csp?isbn=9781449320553* for release details.

ISBN: 978-1-449-32055-3

[LSI]

1344622104

Table of Contents

Preface

The personal computer (PC), which first hit the market over 30 years ago, has undergone tectonic changes that, in turn, launched the PC era. PCs were primarily used in the workplace where software was simple and optimized for use with the keyboard; touching a screen was unheard of until recently. Slowly computers began creeping into the home and many users didn't know what to do with them; they were glorified typewriters.

When PCs started connecting to the Internet, possibilities reached a new level, which had a snowball effect. It allowed academia to share research; it spawned new means of communication from email and online chat to social networking, captivating the minds of people young and old. Soon consumers started using laptops and unplugging from the conventional desktop setting.

This shift had little impact on applications, but helped define a new wave of form factors in phones, tablets, and slates. Eventually, users started demanding more and we ushered in a new era, the modern consumer era. We are all modern consumers, not only consumers of goods, but consumers of information. We are constantly connected through the use of mobile devices as well as more traditional computers. Whatever type of device, be it static or mobile, content is synchronized and up-to-date. These new devices are used as gaming machines and personal entertainment centers, and they are replacing books and magazines for many avid readers.

Today, consumers expect developers to create apps where touch, mobility, and good battery life are a must. Tablets and slates leverage touch as a primary form of interaction while playing a critical role in the adoption of sensors and cameras in everyday computing. They are small and lightweight, making them extremely portable. Devices boot almost instantly so users can get to their content and put them right back in their bag without missing a step. Despite their youth, these devices are being embraced by work forces and consumers worldwide and they appear to be on a relentless progression.

With all this excitement, it's hard to believe we've only begun to scratch the surface. We need a platform built from the ground up with these objectives in mind. This next version of Windows, code-named Windows 8, ships with a new application model for building user experiences tailored to the next generation of devices.

The Windows Runtime

The underpinning for that new user experience is the Windows Runtime. For years Windows desktop applications interacted with the Win32APIs in some fashion, whether they were opening file dialogs, rendering graphics, or communicating over the network. Instead of replacing this, Windows 8 continues its support for the Win32APIs allowing existing Windows 7 apps to run seamlessly. What they built instead is a brand new API from the ground up called the Windows Runtime (WinRT). WinRT consists of an application execution environment and a collection of new APIs, which enables a new line of immersive full screen apps called Windows 8 apps.

Windows desktop applications are still available and continue to be relevant for many situations. In fact, desktop applications can leverage the power of the Windows Runtime API—for example communicating with sensors.

Windows 8 apps are designed to communicate with WinRT via a language-independent projection layer, which enables apps to be written in statically-typed languages like C++, C#, and Visual Basic, while also feeling natural to dynamic languages like JavaScript. WinRT introduces a new trust model for users, called base trust. Unlike full trust, this model isolates each application while funneling high-level action through the runtime broker to ensure users are aware when apps attempt to access protected resources. Even though Windows 8 apps promote a model where the user is in charge, you will find their ability to connect with other apps is far superior than its predecessor. Windows 8 apps can communicate with other apps using generic contracts and send or receive content in various formats—like text and photos. Contracts can also be defined to access core operating system components, like Search, to highlight your app even though it may seem irrelevant. (We'll discuss contracts and search later in Chapter 4.)

 Once a revolutionary technology, like mobile computing, has been unleashed it's hard not to push its potential. You can already see signs that manufacturers and researchers are innovating well beyond what is on the streets today. Microsoft is committed to contributing to the future of technology in a big way and Windows 8 is just the start. For more insight and the impending possibilities into what's next for Microsoft, a video of their vision for the future can be found online at *http://www .youtube.com/playlist?list=PL2B8C6AB94E8259C6*.

Disclaimer

Windows 8 is currently in Release Preview; as such, some of the content in this book may change.

Who This Book Is For

This book is written for existing .NET developers who are interested in the changes introduced with the release of Windows 8.

This book is intended to be a guide to developing complete Windows 8 apps. If you have an idea or you are just curious about the platform, this is the place to start. For a reference on all things related to Windows 8 development I recommend the Windows Dev Center at *http://dev.windows.com* and the Windows Dev Forum at *http://forums .dev.windows.com*.

The samples in this book are in C# and XAML. All of the samples in this book are available for download on this book's website at *http://bendewey.com/getting-started -with-metro-apps* and at *http://bendewey.com/getting-started-with-Windows8-apps*.

How This Book Is Organized

This book focuses on helping you become familiar with the new Windows 8 landscape, WinRT, and writing your first Windows 8 apps, from creating a simple search app to writing a touch enabled app that responds to native sensors. This book will go through the steps taken to create a full application using the Bing Search API and publishing it to the Windows Store. It has been broken up into five chapters:

Chapter 1
> This chapter focuses on a high-level overview of the Windows 8 features that power Windows 8 apps. From the new OS features, like the new Start Screen, to the in app features such as the Application Bar. Many of these features will be covered in depth in later chapters.

Chapter 2
> Before building the full Bing Image Search application I will walk you through creating a simple version of the application that communicates with the Bing Search API and binds the results to a simple UI. If you choose to follow along you will need to obtain an account key for the Bing Search API service on the Azure Marketplace.

Chapter 3
> Once you've seen how to create a simple application using the Bing Search API, I'll show you what it takes to complete an application that leverages the full power of the Windows 8 platform. Chapter 3 will also focus on the goals, techniques, and designs used throughout the app.

Chapter 4
> Developers can create impressive apps of all shapes and sizes. At some point you will need to access some external resource. Whether you're communicating with web services or responding to events from one of the many native sensors, this

chapter shows you how the Bing Image Search application takes advantage of these various features and how to implement them in a maintainable fashion.

Chapter 5

Windows 8 ships with a Windows Store that developers can leverage for marketing and distribution of their apps without having to focus on the nuances of building installers and accepting payments. As you would experience with other app stores, the Windows Store has a certification process. This chapter focuses on navigating that process and the details around app distribution in this new environment.

Conventions Used in This Book

The following typographical conventions are used in this book:

Italic

Indicates new terms, URLs, email addresses, filenames, and file extensions.

`Constant width`

Used for program listings, as well as within paragraphs to refer to program elements such as variable or function names, databases, data types, environment variables, statements, and keywords.

`Constant width bold`

Shows commands or other text that should be touched, clicked, or typed literally by the user.

`Constant width italic`

Shows text that should be replaced with user-supplied values or by values determined by context.

This icon signifies a tip, suggestion, or general note.

This icon indicates a warning or caution.

What You Need to Use This Book

To run the samples from this book, you will need to have a version of Windows 8 Release Preview. I recommend installing to a virtual hard drive (VHD) using the steps laid out by Scott Hanselman at *http://www.hanselman.com/blog/GuideToInstallingAnd BootingWindows8DeveloperPreviewOffAVHDVirtualHardDisk.aspx*.

In addition, you will need a version of Visual Studio 2012 available at *http://www.mi crosoft.com/visualstudio/11*.

Subscribing to the Bing Search API Service on Windows Azure Marketplace

This book uses the free Bing Search API service available from the Windows Azure Marketplace. This Service is a available for anyone to use as long as you register an account and subscribe. In order to use the examples in this book on your own you will need to create an account on the Windows Azure Marketplace and subscribe to the Bing service. This can be setup online by going to *https://datamarket.azure.com/dataset/ 5ba839f1-12ce-4cce-bf57-a49d98d29a44*, signing in with you LiveID by clicking the button in the top right, and then scrolling down and clicking the Sign Up button under the free 5,000 transaction subscription. After you've subscribed, you can click the EX-PLORE THIS DATASET heading to play with the data feed.

Using Code Examples

This book is here to help you get your job done. In general, you may use the code in this book in your programs and documentation. You do not need to contact us for permission unless you're reproducing a significant portion of the code. For example, writing a program that uses several chunks of code from this book does not require permission. Selling or distributing a CD-ROM of examples from O'Reilly books does require permission. Answering a question by citing this book and quoting example code does not require permission. Incorporating a significant amount of example code from this book into your product's documentation does require permission.

We appreciate, but do not require, attribution. An attribution usually includes the title, author, publisher, and ISBN. For example: "*Getting Started with Windows 8 Apps* by Ben Dewey (O'Reilly). Copyright 2012 Ben Dewey, 978-1-449-32055-3.*"

If you feel your use of code examples falls outside fair use or the permission given above, feel free to contact us at *permissions@oreilly.com*.

Safari® Books Online

Safari Books Online (*www.safaribooksonline.com*) is an on-demand digital library that delivers expert content in both book and video form from the world's leading authors in technology and business.

Technology professionals, software developers, web designers, and business and creative professionals use Safari Books Online as their primary resource for research, problem solving, learning, and certification training.

Safari Books Online offers a range of product mixes and pricing programs for organizations, government agencies, and individuals. Subscribers have access to thousands of books, training videos, and prepublication manuscripts in one fully searchable database from publishers like O'Reilly Media, Prentice Hall Professional, Addison-Wesley Professional, Microsoft Press, Sams, Que, Peachpit Press, Focal Press, Cisco Press, John Wiley & Sons, Syngress, Morgan Kaufmann, IBM Redbooks, Packt, Adobe Press, FT Press, Apress, Manning, New Riders, McGraw-Hill, Jones & Bartlett, Course Technology, and dozens more. For more information about Safari Books Online, please visit us online.

How to Contact Us

Please address comments and questions concerning this book to the publisher:

O'Reilly Media, Inc.
1005 Gravenstein Highway North
Sebastopol, CA 95472
800-998-9938 (in the United States or Canada)
707-829-0515 (international or local)
707-829-0104 (fax)

We have a web page for this book, where we list errata, examples, and any additional information. You can access this page at *http://oreil.ly/gs_with_windows_8_apps*.

To comment or ask technical questions about this book, send email to *bookquestions@oreilly.com*.

For more information about our books, courses, conferences, and news, see our website at *http://www.oreilly.com*.

Find us on Facebook: *http://facebook.com/oreilly*

Follow us on Twitter: *http://twitter.com/oreillymedia*

Watch us on YouTube: *http://www.youtube.com/oreillymedia*

How to Contact the Author

Feel free to visit the books website at *http://bendewey.com/getting-started-with-Windows8-apps*. You can also find me on Twitter @bendewey or via email at *ben@nuology.com*.

Acknowledgements

I'd like to thank my employer, Tallan, for its support and for allowing me to attend conferences regularly. I'd also like to thank my editor, Rachel Roumeliotis, and my primary technical reviewer, Mark Freedmean, for putting up with me and the product throughout multiple changes as Windows 8 was a challenging, moving target. Finally, I'd like to thank my family for their undivided support and encouragement throughout the process.

CHAPTER 1

Windows 8: A Quick Tour

When the Windows 8 design language was first announced at MIX 2010, I knew Microsoft was on to something. I really enjoyed the simple use of typography and a focus on content. At the Build conference in September 2011, Microsoft announced its plans to expand the Windows 8 design language to other products, including its flagship product, Microsoft Windows. This release marks a convergence of the latest versions of Windows, Windows Phone, and Xbox where all three use Windows 8 and promote the concept with a trifecta of opportunities that will hopefully complement one another and grow consumer awareness about the collective suite of offerings.

Windows 8 apps are designed primarily for touch interaction, and Windows 8 has been written with this in mind. Microsoft is calling this *the reimagining of Windows*. Everything from the desktop to the start menu has been redesigned and optimized for touch. The Windows Runtime (WinRT), a new application model for running Windows 8 apps, provides access to the new features of the Operating System (OS) and the native hardware capabilities that are available on modern computers, tablets, and slates. This chapter focuses on what it means to reimagine Windows and what's available to help developers reimagine their apps as well.

A User Interface for Touch

In line with other Windows 8–focused technologies like the Windows Phone and Xbox, the main interface for Windows is a vibrant start screen where tiles are used to launch apps. They are big and easily activated on touch devices while providing content that is up-to-date and visible even when flicked across the screen. Unlike desktop apps, Windows 8 apps don't have borders or windows, which are difficult to interact with using touch. Instead they are all full screen, enabling an immersive experience where your apps contain only relevant content. When an app launches in Windows 8, you use specific gestures—swiping in from the bezel on the right or bottom—to activate new touch-based menus. The system menu, or start bar, in conjunction with the Windows Runtime, provides a new model for connecting apps. Once an app is running, you can change settings, search, and share content with other apps without having to leave the full screen experience.

Start Screen

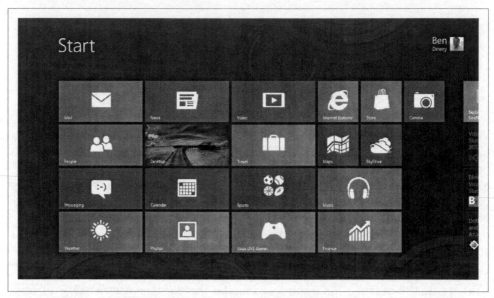

Figure 1-1. The new Start Screen that powers Windows 8 apps in Windows

The new Windows 8 start screen, shown in Figure 1-1, provides a fast and fluid way to interact with all your important content. From checking email or the latest news, glancing at the weather or your stocks, checking in with your friends on various social networks, or just listening to music, the start screen keeps you updated on your life. This means no bouncing between apps and the home screen just to check statuses.

Tiles make up the start screen with their bright colors and clean text. They can be organized into groups and personalized for each user. Simply tapping a tile launches the app in a full screen view. Apps can have either small or wide tiles in a number of different styles, providing clean and exciting animation. In addition to the primary application tile, apps can define additional tiles. For example, the weather app might show its tile with information from your hometown in New York. Before going on vacation, you can add a secondary tile for your destination of London. The secondary tile can provide live information about the weather in London, and when you tap the tile, the weather app will launch directly into a detailed view of London's weather.

By default, start screen settings are stored in the cloud, which allows the layout of your tiles to be consistent across all devices. Using the pinch gesture for zooming out, you can get a broad glance at your start screen and see a list of all the application groups.

With this new user interface come many new features and ways to interact with Windows. In conjunction with the new start screen comes a brand new start bar, which allows users to get back to the start screen or communicate with other components of Windows or the other apps installed on the system.

Start Bar

The start button has been a keystone of Windows for many releases. It has undergone numerous changes, but this one is by far the most drastic: Microsoft has replaced the start button with a Start Bar, which is the hub of inter-app connectivity. In addition to the typical Windows logo that will return you to the start screen, the Start Bar contains charms. Regardless of which app is running, you can use *charms* to access common features such as searching and modifying settings. You can also use the Share and Devices charms to quickly send content to other apps or hardware such as your printer. To display the Start Bar, simply swipe your finger in from the right side of the screen and it will slide into place.

With the Start Bar visible, you will see an overlay with system status information on the lower-left side. It displays notifications, network and battery monitors, and the current date and time (see Figure 1-2). The Start Bar, on the right side, contains the Windows logo and four charms.

 When using a mouse, take advantage of the screen's corner features. Move your mouse to the top right corner and it the Start Bar will appear. If you prefer keyboard shortcuts: Windows key + C will show the Start Bar.

Each of these charms are as follows:

Search

Windows has merged the All Programs list and the File System search into a common UI for searching everything on your computer (see Figure 1-3). The same interface for displaying apps is used to provide search throughout the Windows experience. You can search for apps, files, settings, and any information provided by your installed apps.

 When using a keyboard, you can just start typing on the start screen to search for an app. If you are in an app, you can click the Windows key and then start typing.

Figure 1-2. New Windows Start Bar slides in from the right side

Share

Share provides a way to send data to other applications without having to leave the app. Early samples treat this as an alternative to traditional copy-and-paste methods; examples include posting to Facebook, Twitter, or sending email, but the possibilities are endless.

Devices

Devices allows apps to communicate with the computer's hardware. The initial examples include printing, projecting, and sending content to your Xbox, other device, and/or USB hard drives. Device manufacturers can communicate with apps in ways that are relevant to a particular device. Screens for this section will typically be developed by device manufacturers. For example, your printer will have specific screens for its use.

Settings

Settings is split into two sections: system settings and app settings. System settings contain quick access to networking, volume, screen, notifications, power, and keyboard. App settings depend on the app and developers should determine what settings are relevant to their apps.

Windows Programming Reimagined

The Win32 APIs have been a core component to native Windows programming for over 15 years. In addition to all the changes to Windows, Microsoft is reimagining the

Figure 1-3. New Windows Search offers a replacement view for All Programs

way in which programs, or apps, are written. Windows 8 apps can be written using the following languages:

- JavaScript and HTML5/CSS3
- C# and XAML
- VB.NET and XAML
- C++ and XAML
- C++ with DirectX
- Hybrid

All of the languages above are designed to be first class citizens. This means that no matter what language you choose, you will have equivalent capabilities. At this point, the decision of which language to use is strongly guided by the preferences of the team. Regardless of the choice you make, all Windows 8 apps communicate with the new Native Application Programming Interface (API) called the Windows Runtime, or just WinRT for short.

A New Native API: The Windows Runtime

Windows 8 apps are based on a new application model that has been completely re-written from the ground up. While the Win32 APIs were written for C, WinRT APIs written in C++ and designed to be object oriented. This gives the APIs the flexibility to be used by multiple languages. Everything that is needed to host an application and communicate with the operating system has been updated or rewritten in native C++ and is exposed out via an API Metadata format (*.winmd* file).

This consistent framework allows the API to be optimized for performance. File access can be centralized and made consistent across all languages. User interface components can be hardware accelerated and common animations can become easily accessible. Resource management is handled at a higher level and currently running applications can be confident that they will be given additional resources if the system experiences pressure. In total, this gives users a better experience.

Language Support

Between the different languages and the new WinRT APIs is a layer called the projection layer. This layer maintains the proxies and handles the activation of WinRT objects. For C# developers, this means no more P/Invoke. Write the C# code just like regular code. While WinRT is designed for use with JavaScript, C#, Visual Basic, and C++, this book will focus on C#. The techniques are often the same and the syntax is surprisingly similar considering they are different languages.

JavaScript

Windows 8 apps leverage the Internet Explorer WebHost, to render HTML5/CSS3, and the Chakra JavaScript engine to execute native web apps. These apps are as flexible as existing web apps, but they can perform tasks previously available only to desktop applications—tasks like using the camera to take a picture, accessing the accelerometer to determine the tilt of a device during game play, or reading and writing to a file on the local filesystem. In addition, JavaScript apps can communicate with other apps on the OS, as a source or a target of information, and provide interactive tiles and secondary tiles.

C# and Visual Basic

Existing WPF or Silverlight developers might wonder why the name changed to C# or Visual Basic and XAML and the answer comes from the addition of C++ and XAML. If you wanted to expose all of XAML to C++ as a UI technology, it wouldn't make much sense to spin up the CLR just to parse and render some XAML only to revert back to C++ for the remainder of your code execution. The only logical answer is to push XAML down further in the stack and expose it out through the same projection layer that is used for other Windows Runtime objects. This means that the XAML consumed from these Windows 8 apps is now written in C++. Although many of the XAML controls and binding techniques remain, there are slight differences, and it is a complete rewrite in a completely new language after all.

For developers who are familiar with .NET, you'll find many of the APIs and libraries will still be available. Microsoft has created a new profile called the .NET Profile for Windows Windows 8 apps. Like the .NET Client profile, this is a subset of the full .NET

Framework that is specific to Windows 8 apps. In the process, they've removed duplicate and legacy code; optimized APIs for multiple core machines and asynchronous development; and hardware accelerated the UI layer. There may be new APIs to learn on the WinRT side, but .NET developers should find the developer experience extremely familiar.

You can think of this change as if Microsoft took Silverlight or WPF and cut it in half. The XAML UI and application hosting controls were moved into the Windows Runtime with many brand new native Windows features. The remainder of the .NET components have been moved to this new .NET Profile for Windows Windows 8 apps.

C++

Microsoft has made changes to C++ in the past to make it compatible with managed languages, and they continue to do so with WinRT. There were similar challenges in order to cooperate with WinRT, but unlike the managed C++, developers need a way to transition between native and managed C++. Windows 8 comes with a new C++ compiler switch (/cx) that enables the C++ Compiler Extensions. This exposes typical managed concepts, such as reference objects, partial classes, and generics, but allows easy portability between their native counterparts.

 The WinRT libraries themselves are written through the same C++ extensions made available to C++ developers. Objects that are projected out to other languages use a managed wrapper object, which points to the same memory as the native objects.

Hosted Application Model

Each Windows 8 app is loaded into a new application host. The most important responsibility is resource management. The way Windows ensures that the current app has the necessary resources available is by closing down other apps when needed.

The two main resources that apps typically consume are CPU cycles and memory. These shutdowns are handled separately. First to be taken care of are the CPU cycles; shortly after an app has left the foreground, it receives an event signaling itself to deactivate. This is the last chance to save state or consume the CPU, and this must be handled in a timely fashion. This is called tombstoning and from here the app is in a suspended state. The second step occurs when your system is low on memory. In this case, Windows will terminate the app without notification to free up memory. Developers can gain some startup performance if they realize that their app is not always terminated and they retain items in a cache. More information on tombstoning can be found in Chapter 3.

Single File Deployment

In the process of reimagining Windows, the application model, and the application programming interfaces (APIs), Microsoft overhauled the deployment process. This is the first time that Microsoft has allowed native apps to be installed from a single file. This file, or deployment package, is an *.appx* (pronounced App-X) file.

This new deployment process includes incremental updates. They support side-by-side installs of different versions for multiple users. Each application package is digitally signed with a certificate and hashes are created and verified for each app before execution. More information about .appx packages can be found in Chapter 5.

Windows Store

Getting your app to market and in front of Windows' large install base is simple with the integrated Windows Store. In order to have apps published in the Windows Store, developers will have to submit apps for certification. Certification will verify code for a number of different conditions, such as invalid access to protected APIs, the use of proper capabilities, and proper handling of exceptions. More information about the Windows Store can be found in Chapter 5.

Inside Windows 8 Apps

The Windows Runtime provides a simple model for building apps of any type or design. However, in order to make a cohesive experience for all users, Microsoft is promoting a few design concepts that you should follow when building apps. These concepts include designing with typography, placing the back button in a consistent location, using the Application Bar, and providing elegant animation. Windows 8 apps come with built-in support libraries and controls for these, so implementation is simplified.

Application Bar

With full screen apps and the lack of chrome on the windows, interfaces lose menu bars. These are the links you typically see at the top that say File, Tools, Help, etc. Windows 8 apps have included a new Application Bar that is meant to provide application-specific buttons. When the user swipes a finger up from the bottom bezel, it slides into place just like the Start Bar, but from the bottom instead (see Figure 1-4).

 To activate the application bar with a mouse, just right-click or click Windows key + Z on the keyboard.

Figure 1-4. Weather app sample in Windows 8 showing the Application Bar

Application Bars are optional and completely customizable. Many apps are built so the Application Bar varies based on the context of the current page. The checklist for designing Application Bars is available at *http://msdn.microsoft.com/en-us/library/windows/apps/hh465302(v=VS.85).aspx*; it recommends right-aligning commands that vary in the app bar and left-aligning all the buttons that are consistent throughout the application.

 Application settings do not belong on the Application Bar and should leverage the Settings charm on the Start Bar. More information about the Settings charm will be described later in Chapter 3.

Semantic Zoom

Anyone who has used a touch device is familiar with the pinch and stretch gestures used for zooming. This gesture has typically been used for zooming images, maps, or applications that have a functional requirement for zooming. Microsoft is trying to prove that almost every app can benefit from this semantic zoom. For example, if you have a list with hundreds of items, you can pinch your fingers on the screen, change the icon size, and get a view that provides more items than a standard list. Semantic zoom must be something that you decide to incorporate into your app, since it does not work by default. The sample app from the Build conference provides a great example: by simply pinching on the schedule of sessions you can change the list from a full view to a high level glance of all days (see Figure 1-5 and Figure 1-6).

The Windows Runtime provides built-in controls for SemanticZoom. This control has two zoom levels a ZoomedInView and a ZoomedOutView. To implement the control you provide a custom GridView or ListView for each view.

Figure 1-5. Sample app from the Build conference in full view

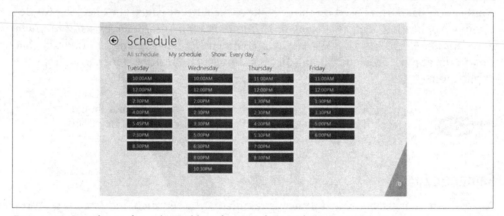

Figure 1-6. Sample app from the Build conference after pinching to zoom out

Animation

In order to build rich user experiences in your Windows 8 apps, consider the proper use of animation. Regardless of the language used, traditional forms of animation are still available, such as DOM manipulation in JavaScript, or storyboards in XAML. In addition, Windows 8 apps come with support for some common animations and transition.

In XAML-based applications, you can use ThemeTransitions. These are provided by the Windows Runtime and as with any XAML control, you can create your own transitions or use one of the built in ones listed in Table 1-1.

Table 1-1. A list of WinRT XAML animations from Windows.UI.Xaml.Media.Animation

Methods	Descriptions
EntranceThemeTransition	Provides a subtle animation to slide content into place as it enters the UI
RepositionThemeTransition	Animates any change to an item's position
AddDeleteThemeTransition	Provides animation for when items get added/removed to a parent panel
ContentThemeTransition	Animates changes to the Content property of an element
ReorderThemeTransition	Animates the changes to a panel in response to filtering and sorting children

For a full list of XAML animations see *http://msdn.microsoft.com/en-us/library/windows/apps/br243232.aspx*.

Animations will not be covered in depth in this book. For more information about animation using XAML you can find separate documentation at *http://msdn.microsoft.com/en-us/library/windows/apps/hh452703.aspx*.

Outside Your App

Almost every application needs to communicate with the Internet or devices in some fashion. Windows also contains numerous features that any compelling app will likely leverage. While the previous sections focused on the new features of Windows and the application development platform, this section focuses on the new features specific to Windows 8 apps and how they communicate with functionality outside the app.

The tiles on the new start screen can be updated periodically to provide important details regarding your app. Apps can send and receive information from various open contracts allowing them to get content from a web of other apps on the users' system that are unknown to developers at design time. Implementing these features appropriately adds to the users' experience when they use your app, and creates a better web of collective apps for users.

Tiles

Every Windows 8 app comes with a primary tile. Developers must provide an image for every application to be used as the default tile. This tile is displayed until the application is launched and an update is sent. The default tile has to be a static image (150x150 for square tiles, and 310x150 for wide tiles). Once an update is sent, the tile becomes a Live Tile. Depending on the app, it may highlight an upcoming appointment, the weather in the neighborhood, or the latest sports scores for a favorite team. These apps are providing information even when they are not active.

In addition to a primary tile, you can create multiple secondary tiles for your app. The difference is that secondary tiles can link to a specific page or section in your app, a process called "deep linking."

Pickers

Due to the multitude of viruses, malicious software, and the like in the wild, Microsoft has tried to thwart these attempts by disabling raw access to the filesystem. WinRT provides a feature called pickers. Pickers come in a variety of forms, such as FilePickers, FolderPickers, and ContactPickers. They provide the functionality of a typical file dialog box, except that they also can expose content from third party apps. If your app has data relevant to these pickers, you can provide a contract that allows your app to provide data to any other app that uses the same file picker. Figure 1-7 shows a file picker of images. Notice the Socialite app (Socialite is a Facebook demo) listed in the menu. This allows you to pick images from your photos that were previously uploaded to Facebook.

Charms

A big challenge in current Windows development is sharing content between applications. Pickers do a lot to help this, but let's say you wanted to share a link from a news article with all of your Twitter followers. This was possible in Windows 7, but it caused an abrupt context switch. You copied the link into your clipboard, started the Twitter client, switched applications, pasted the link, shared the content, and then you could switch back to your previous task. In Windows 8, you can simply activate the start bar, choose the Share charm, select a Twitter client, and click share without ever having to leave the application.

Apps can define capabilities that allow them to be both sources and targets for charms. More information on charms can be found in Chapter 4.

Sensors and Devices

Windows 8 is packaged with support for more sensors and devices because of new devices like tablets and mobile computing. The sample tablet from the Build conference has a forward and rear facing camera, an accelerometer, a GPS, and even a near field communication card. As a developer, you have access to use them for any application.

The Windows Runtime includes APIs for communicating with all kinds of hardware. Some of these devices may be relevant only to tablets. Regardless, these APIs make communication with these devices easier than ever before. They provide consistency and access to raw, native features so complex algorithms and streaming servers are not required.

More information about sensors and devices can be found in Chapter 4.

Figure 1-7. File Picker showing a drop-down menu with custom apps (Socialite)

Summary

You have been given a glimpse of what is in store for you as you begin to develop for Windows 8. This is one of the biggest releases for Microsoft in some time, with enhancements to ensure a safe and optimal experience for the user. I hope this book will show you how writing Windows 8 apps can be a pleasurable experience for developers as well. Maybe your app will be the next featured app on the Windows Store, with downloads beyond your expectations.

CHAPTER 2

Getting Started

Where Is the Hello World app?

Rather than show you a simple Hello World app, which is good at teaching syntax but not much else, I'll be building a practical app that can be used throughout the book. This allows me to progressively build on the examples and use the native features of Windows 8 in a complete system.

 All kidding aside, if you want a Hello World app, see the Getting Started Guide on the Windows Developer Center at *http://msdn.microsoft.com/ library/windows/apps/br211386*.

Microsoft's Bing, like many popular search engines, provides a service for retrieving its results. This service has recently been migrated to the Windows Azure Marketplace and is perfect for showing the power of Windows 8 apps. It allows me to communicate with a free online service and demonstrate how to search, share, update tiles, and much more with a vast collection of images.

I'll create a simple version first that is a single page application with a textbox and a button to execute the search. When the user clicks the search button, the app loads the results from the web service, attaches them to a listbox, and displays the results (see Figure 2-1).

Before you start building the app, let me take a moment to describe the Bing Search API so you can become familiar with the results format.

Bing Search API

In the Preface, I outlined the steps to subscribe to the Bing Search API service on the Windows Azure Marketplace. Once you've subscribed for the service, you can explore the data in the API using the DataMarket service explorer. This tool is available from

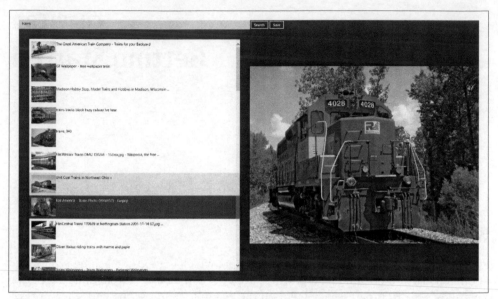

Figure 2-1. Bing Search App

the Bing Search API service home page by clicking the Explore This Dataset link. Figure 2-2 shows a screenshot of the tool after searching for Trains.

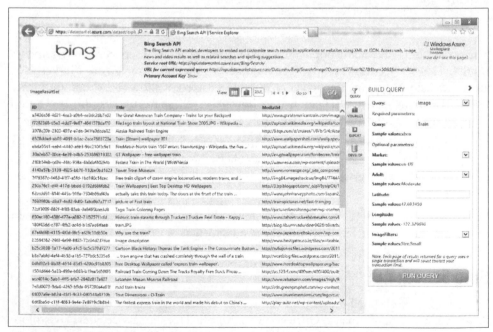

Figure 2-2. Results from Bing image search for train using the DataMarket service explorer

This page provides you with five important pieces of information:

- The available options for the Query
- The resulting data format and fields
- The Service root URL
- The URL for current expressed query
- The Primary Account Key associated to the logged in user

These items should be noted or recorded somewhere so you can refer to them throughout the remainder of the book.

In addition to providing a UI for exploring the service, the Windows Azure Marketplace provides code that can be used within your .NET application to access the data. If you navigate back to the Bing Search API landing page by clicking on the logo in the top left, you will see a link to download a .NET C# Class Library, which is a single *.cs* file that you can include in your application (see Figure 2-3).

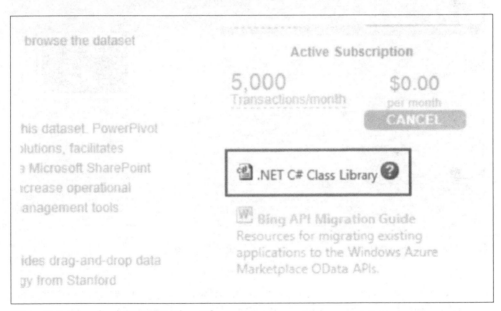

Figure 2-3. Download .NET C# Class Library

The Bing Search API supports two formats at the moment. The first is an XML-based ATOM format, which will be used by the C# class that was just downloaded. In addition, the API supports a JSON format, which can easily be used by any HTML and JavaScript app. The documentation on the Windows Azure Marketplace contains more information about these formats, or you can put the URL for the current query into any web browser, providing your Primary Account Key as your username and password. This will return the results in their raw form.

Getting Started: The BingSimpleSearch App

If you've ever created a new project in Visual Studio, you already know how to get started creating Windows 8 apps. To begin, open Visual Studio 2012 on a Windows 8 machine, and select File→New→Project. Figure 2-4 shows the full list of templates available for Windows Windows 8 apps. Each language contains a similar list of templates for creating Windows 8 apps. Select Blank App (XAML) under the Visual C#→Windows Store folder, enter the name BingSimpleSearch, and click OK.

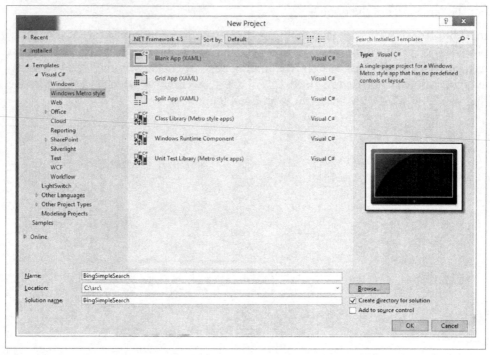

Figure 2-4. New Project Dialog

Now that you have created a new project, open Solution Explorer (View→Solution Explorer). You should see the files from Figure 2-5.

The empty application template for Windows 8 apps contains two XAML files. Both of these files contain an associated code-behind file (i.e., a file with the same name with the addition of .cs).

App.xaml

> *App.xaml* is the application entry point for your project. This simple application just loads the MainPage. As an application evolves, this file can be used for initializing your application dependencies (e.g., an inversion of control container), handling tombstoning and saving of settings, and providing activation triggers.

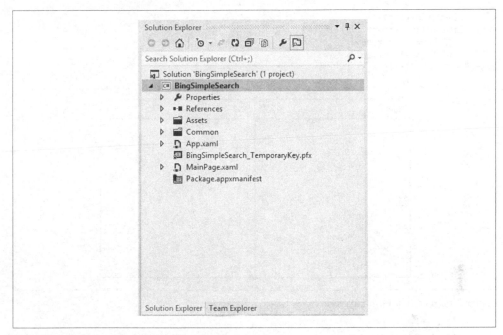

Figure 2-5. Solution Explorer for New Project

MainPage.xaml

>*MainPage.xaml* is the primary view for the application, and it contains no content by default. As an application evolves, this file would likely contain a `Frame` control (*http://msdn.microsoft.com/en-US/library/windows/apps/windows.ui.xaml.controls .frame*), which allows your app to provide navigation between multiple pages. It would also be used as the primary shell of the UI for your apps global items like settings.

Open up the *MainPage.xaml* file and you will see the initial XAML content provided by the template. This is where you will be adding the `TextBox` and the `Button` to perform your searching. Scroll down to the root grid (it should have a `Background` set to the `ApplicationPageBackgroundBrush` resource). Before you add the textbox and the button, you are going to layout the grid's columns and rows as in Figure 2-6.

To do this, you need two rows and two columns. The two columns will be evenly spaced at 50% and 50%. The two rows, on the other hand, will be set up to provide only the minimum amount of space required for the textbox, and the remaining space will be allocated to the ListBox (as seen in Figure 2-6). The XAML for the grid layout definition would look like Example 2-1.

Example 2-1. Definition of Grid Layout

```
<Grid.RowDefinitions>
        <RowDefinition Height="Auto" />
        <RowDefinition />
```

```
</Grid.RowDefinitions>
<Grid.ColumnDefinitions>
        <ColumnDefinition />
        <ColumnDefinition />
</Grid.ColumnDefinitions>
```

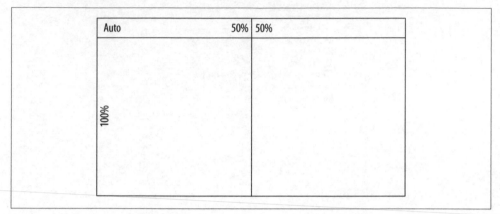

Figure 2-6. Sketch of Grid Layout

Immediately following the row and column definitions, add a `TextBox` and a `Button` like in Example 2-2.

Example 2-2. TextBox and Button for use with search app

```
<TextBox x:Name="SearchQuery" />
<Button Content="Search" Grid.Column="1" Click="Search_Click" />
```

Notice that you are providing a name to the textbox so that it can be accessed from the code-behind later. In addition, you need to supply the row and column assignments only if they are not equal to 0. The textbox is defaulted to `Grid.Row="0"` and `Grid.Col umn="0"`. On the button there is a Click event assignment to `Search_Click`, which maps to a method called `Search_Click` on the code-behind where the Bing search code will be written (see Example 2-3). To access the code-behind, click the arrow next to *Main-Page.xaml* in the Solution Explorer and open the file *MainPage.xaml.cs*.

Example 2-3. Search event on the code-behind for handling the Bing web service call

```
private async void Search_Click(object sender, RoutedEventArgs e)
{
        // Put webservice code here
}
```

Communicating with a web service may take longer than 50ms. Because of that, WinRT requires that this be an asynchronous operation. In .NET, you can use the new `async/await` keywords. These new keywords allow you to write your asynchronous code as if it were synchronous and the compiler handles the transferring of data between different threads. You will notice later in Example 2-5, the `await` keyword is used to unwrap the `Task<T>` object from an async method. For example, if you have an asynchronous method that returns a `Task<string>`, calling that method with an `await` keyword will result in just a `string`. Despite the fact that the code in the example reads as a synchronous call, and debugs like one, under the covers it's actually triggering a continuation in which case the method gets split into two: the code before the await and the code after the await. For more information about the new async and await keywords, see *http://msdn.microsoft.com/en-us/library/win dows/apps/hh452713.aspx*.

Bing Search API Service class

In the previous section, I showed you the download link for the service classes provided by the Windows Azure Marketplace. Now that you've created your project you can add this file to your project.

In addition, you will need to add references to `Microsoft.Data.OData.Metro` and `Micro soft.Data.Service.Client.Metro`. To do so, you can right-click the References in the Solution Explorer and click Add Reference. From here, you can click the Browse button on the bottom, navigate to *C:\Program Files (x86)\Microsoft WCF Data Services\5.0\bin \Metro*, and select both *Microsoft.Data.OData.Metro.dll* and *Microsoft.Data.Services.Client.Metro.dll*. Finally, click OK.

This file, and the references, contain everything you need to connect from a .NET application. The only thing it's missing is support for the latest asynchronous features in .NET 4.5. To add this, create a new class called *BingSearchContainerExtensions.cs*. Place the code from Example 2-4 into this new file.

Example 2-4. Async extensions for BingSearchContainer

```
using System.Collections.Generic;
using System.Data.Services.Client;
using System.Threading.Tasks;

namespace Bing
{
    public static class BingSearchContainerExtensions
    {
        public static Task<IEnumerable<T>> ExecuteAsync<T>(
            this DataServiceQuery<T> query)
        {
            return Task.Factory.FromAsync<IEnumerable<T>>(
                query.BeginExecute, query.EndExecute, null);
```

```
        }
    }
}
```

Calling the Bing Search API

Now that the code is included and WCF Data Services are ready to communicate with our Windows Azure Marketplace endpoint the code is very straightforward. Example 2-5 shows the updated `Search_Click` method. In this method, I created a new `BingSearchContainer` with the *Service root URL* from the previous section, and provide my Primary Account key as the `Credentials`. From here, you can use one of the many methods provided by the download service file. In this case, you want images so you use the `Image` method and supply the necessary parameters. Finally, call the new async extension method, which executes the call to the web service and when it completes, you can update the UI with the resulting objects.

Example 2-5. WCF Data Services call to get search results

```
// add 'using Bing;'
// add 'using System.Net;'

private async void Search_Click(object sender, RoutedEventArgs e)
{
        string accountKey = "<AccountKey>";

        var context = new BingSearchContainer(
                new Uri("https://api.datamarket.azure.com/Data.ashx/Bing/Search"));
        context.Credentials = new NetworkCredential(accountKey, accountKey);

        var result = await context.Image(this.SearchQuery.Text,
                "en-US", null, null, null, null).ExecuteAsync();
        ImagesList.ItemsSource = result.ToList();
}
```

Wrapping Up the UI

The final piece is to bind the visual elements. In Example 2-5, you set the results to an ImagesList `ListBox` that had not been created yet. On the `ListBox`, you will need to specify a `DataTemplate` for how to visually represent the model, which in this case is just a single image. Example 2-6 shows the `ListBox` definition and should be placed in the *MainPage.xaml* file directly under the search button.

Example 2-6. ListBox with a DataTemplate for an image result

```
<ListBox x:Name="ImagesList" Margin="40" Grid.Row="1">
    <ListBox.ItemTemplate>
        <DataTemplate>
            <StackPanel Orientation="Horizontal">
                <Image Source="{Binding Thumbnail.MediaUrl}" Width="100" />
                <TextBlock Text="{Binding Title}" />
            </StackPanel>
```

```
        </DataTemplate>
      </ListBox.ItemTemplate>
</ListBox>
```

We are also going to add two images mapped to the thumbnail and the full-size image on the right-hand column. This will give you the typical effect of an image appearing pixelated while loading and becoming sharper once the download of the full-size image completes. For this effect, stack the images on top of each other; since they are the same aspect ratio, it will show the thumbnail and then cover it up with the full-size image (see Example 2-7). Although the only requirement is that this code is at the same level as the other items in the Grid, I recommend placing this code below the ListBox.

Example 2-7. Large screen image bound to selected item of the ListBox

```
<Grid Grid.Row="1" Grid.Column="1">
    <Image Source="{Binding SelectedItem.Thumbnail.MediaUrl, ElementName=ImagesList}" />
    <Image Source="{Binding SelectedItem.MediaUrl, ElementName=ImagesList}" />
</Grid>
```

You may also notice the usage of the `ElementName` binding in Example 2-7. This is telling the app to access our model through the `ListBox`'s `SelectedItem` property.

Running the BingSimpleSearch App

Your patience is about to be rewarded. You can click Run (the play button) in Visual Studio and your app will build, deploy (install on your Windows 8 Start Screen), and launch. Now you can enter whatever search term you desire, and the ListBox will populate with the thumbnails. If you select one of the images, the full-size image will populate on the right-hand side of the screen, as shown in Figure 2-7.

This is a simple example that just creates a few controls, uses C# to access a web service, parses the results, and then displays that data to the user using a `ListBox` control. With the exception of the XAML controls, all of the code is written with the .NET Profile for Windows 8 Apps. What I'd really like to do is leverage the new features of WinRT, which are found under the `Windows.*` namespace.

Unlocking WinRT (the FileSavePicker)

This app allows access to full screen images that the user may want to download. With Windows 8 apps and WinRT there is no need to download the file in a web browser sense, because you can write directly to the filesystem by requesting a file using the new `FileOpenPicker`. Just like the search event handler, we need to add a button to allow the user to save the image. Replace the XAML for the Search `Button` from the earlier, with the code from Example 2-8.

Figure 2-7. Bing SimpleSearch in action

Example 2-8. Save Button used to trigger the FileSavePicker

```
<StackPanel Grid.Column="1" Orientation="Horizontal">
        <Button Content="Search" Click="Search_Click" />
        <Button Content="Save" Click="Save_Click" />
        <TextBlock x:Name="Status" Style="{StaticResource BasicTextStyle}" />
</StackPanel>
```

Basically, I've taken the Search `Button` and wrapped it into a `StackPanel` so all the elements line up in a row. Then I added the new Save `Button`, which points to a new event handler in the code-behind. Finally, I added a new `TextBlock` to display a status when saving the image.

To wire up the code for the Save `Button`, I have to add the code in the code-behind. Example 2-9 shows the code needed to download the file when the Save `Button` is clicked.

Example 2-9. Event Handler for the Save Button

```
// add 'using System;'
// add 'using Windows.Networking.BackgroundTransfer;'
// add 'using Windows.Storage.Pickers;'

private async void Save_Click(object sender, RoutedEventArgs e)
{
        var image = ImagesList.SelectedItem as ImageResult;
        if (image == null) return;

        var uri = new Uri(image.MediaUrl);
        var filename = uri.Segments[uri.Segments.Length - 1];
```

```
    var extension = System.IO.Path.GetExtension(filename);

    var picker = new FileSavePicker();
    picker.SuggestedFileName = filename;
    picker.SuggestedStartLocation = PickerLocationId.PicturesLibrary;
    picker.FileTypeChoices.Add(extension.Trim('.').ToUpper(),
                    new string[] { extension });

    var saveFile = await picker.PickSaveFileAsync();
    if (saveFile != null)
    {
            Status.Text = "Download Started";
            var download = new BackgroundDownloader().CreateDownload(uri, saveFile);
            await download.StartAsync();
            Status.Text = "Download Complete";
    }
}
```

The event handler does two basic things that use the new WinRT APIs. First, it defines and displays the `FileSavePicker` for the user to select a file. Then it saves the file using the `BackgroundDownloader` API.

I could simply call the `FileSavePicker` with no arguments, but that would require the user to create the proper file extension without providing any hints to the user: not a very good user experience. On the other hand, I can take the filename from the URL and provide both the name and the extension as hints to the user. Before I created the `FileSavePicker`, I took a simple approach to parsing the filename and extensions from the URL. Now the `FileSavePicker` can be created and I can specify the suggested information. Call `picker.PickSaveFileAsync()`, which launches the `FileSavePicker` UI; the user is blocked until he selects a file or clicks cancel. In the event that the user cancels that UI, then the `saveFile` will be null; otherwise, I can take the file and write to it.

The second part of the event handler creates a new `BackgroundDownloader` and tells it to create a new `DownloadOperation` based on the URL and the file selected from the `FileSavePicker`. You can do a number of things with this `DownloadOperation`, like support larger files, support metered connections, and provide progress and cancellation support. In this case the images are fairly small, so just start the download and update the `Status.Text` property with a before and after status. For more information about the `BackgroundDownload` API, you can download a sample at *http://code.msdn.microsoft.com/windowsapps/Background-Transfer-Sample-d7833f61*.

If you run the app again, you will see a new button to save the image. If you perform a search, select an image, and click Save, you will see the `FileSavePicker`. The picker and the `BackgroundDownloader` are full WinRT APIs and are specific to this new platform. This is just a taste of some of the new APIs that are available.

Summary

If you've been following along, you've already created a nice simple app. So far we've created a new UI in XAML, used C# for communication over the network with a web service, and communicated with WinRT to provide direct file access based on the user's selection. The next few chapters will expand on this information and show more examples of how to use WinRT in a number of different places.

CHAPTER 3

Application Architecture

The Bing Image Search App

In order to have a fully functioning app and eventually publish it to the Windows Store, you will need to properly handle application state while also considering the user's bandwidth, disk space, and other system resources. I've simplified this to what I would call being a developer good citizen of the platform. This means providing users with an optimal experience regardless of the device or the presence of network connectivity. Whether you value user experience or not, Microsoft has a set of guidelines that must be followed to pass certification for the Windows Store. These guidelines value user experience, and if you plan to release your app through the Windows Store, you should consider these guidelines from the beginning. For more information on what's required by the Windows Store, see Chapter 5.

This chapter describes core components of a more complex application than the Bing Simple Search app we explored in the previous chapter. These concepts will be used throughout the book, and I will reference various aspects of the application through the use of these techniques. If you are familiar with previous XAML-based technologies, you will likely be familiar with these concepts. As a reminder, all the code for the book's full application is available online at *https://github.com/bendewey/GettingStartedWith MetroApps*. I encourage you to download the code ahead of time so you can follow along.

Goals

Before I get too deep into the code, let's step back and review the goals of the Bing Image Search app (Figure 3-1).

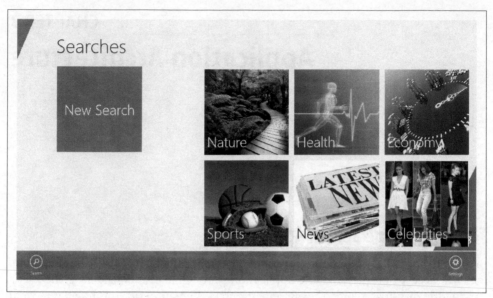

Figure 3-1. Bing Image Search App

Usability

Usability goals determine the way users interact with the app, from how quickly they can use it to how satisfied they are with the experience. In my case, usability, functionality, and interface design goals are all synonymous.

Allow users to search, browse, save, and share images
The Bing Image Search app will use the Bing Search API to retrieve a list of search results and display them in a number of different user-friendly views.

Make use of the charms where applicable (search, share, settings)
The Windows 8 charms provide a nice way to perform many tasks that are common to all applications. A goal of this app is to use charms where ever applicable. This does not mean that you should rely on the charms for all user interaction; in contrast, I encourage you to provide app bar buttons that trigger the charm panes and provide users with an alternative to opening the charms to discover critical pieces of your app like search.

Expose the content to other apps via the file pickers
Windows 8 provides new and improved file pickers that can load images from numerous locations, not only the local filesystem. The Bing Image Search app should allow users from other apps to select images for use within their app.

Should support multiple layouts
In addition to multiple screen resolutions, you will need to consider how your application will respond to changes in orientation (portrait and landscape) and how it will look in the new Snapped mode. Many of the Visual Studio application

templates, use a `LayoutAwarePage` base class to provide pages with updates to their state. The Bing Image Search application will use the same technique to notify its pages of any changes.

Use gestures and sensors to provide users with unique ways to interact with the app
While a button to load more results is sufficient, it's becoming common for tablets and slates to support a shake gesture for reloading content. In order to be on the cutting edge, the Bing Image Search app should support these gestures.

Non-functional

Non-functional goals describe what the app should be; this is in contrast to what the app should *do*, as discussed in the previous section. This also includes features that may not be encountered during typical application use, but would ultimately affect the user experience.

Be a good citizen on the platform
To be a good citizen means to do all you can to ensure a good user experience. This means your app should be responsive and clean. A good experience in the app is not the only concern. Being a good citizen also includes sparing use of network bandwidth and isolated storage so that your app does not hog system resources.

Should gracefully respond to the user when network access is disabled
Since it's not practical to store all the possible image results from the Bing Search API, the app can't offer the users a compelling offline experience. If your app has the ability to provide valid data to the user when offline, then I encourage you to consider this goal for yourself. Simply informing the users that the app is not available when the user is offline will suffice.

Should support a loading progress bar and downloading indicators
Because all the data for the Bing Image Search app comes from online sources, the network traffic can be quite heavy. For this reason, it's imperative to provide progress bars and status information to the user so they know when the app is busy. The main `Shell` of the application exposes status update functionality through an `IStatusService` interface.

Should gracefully handle exception messages
The Bing Image Search app should never return sensitive information regarding exceptions to users. To handle this, the `DialogService` class can be used throughout the app or as unhandled exceptions are encountered, it can provide users with friendly error messages.

Should perform all actions asynchronously
WinRT does not provide any way to perform actions that take longer than 50ms without using an asynchronous pattern. The Bing Image Search app maintains this requirement and performs all long-running tasks asynchronously so the user experience is never jeopardized.

Development Process Goals

While the previous two goals relate to the overall user experience, development process goals impact developers and the overall code maintainability throughout the lifetime of the application.

Bing Image Search should have highly testable code.

The Bing Image Search uses the Model-View-ViewModel (MVVM) pattern to provide testable application logic. ViewModels are provided to their respective Views via the `ViewModelLocator`. All of the ViewModels and services are instantiated via a central Inversion of Control (IoC) container and dependencies are provided to their objects via Dependency Injection (DI). This allows the unit tests to provide mock implementations when testing functionality.

Bing Image Search should adapt to the application for compatibility with new capabilities of future versions.

The Bing Image Search app has an `ApplicationSettings` class that is a strongly typed wrapper over application storage. The underlying implementation remains flexible to change. In the event that you need to change whether settings are roaming, local, or serialized to a file, the object exposed to the consuming classes remains unchanged.

Bing Image Search wants to handle all events in a centralized location, be it Windows events or local app events.

The Bing Image Search app uses a `MessageHub` to handle messages. Messages are used to signal the occurrence of an event in a loosely coupled fashion. Messages are made up of two parts: an `IMessage`, which is the payload, and an `IHandler`, which is responsible for handling the message when it is sent. There is also an `IMessagePump`, which is responsible for listening to events like a search action or a share data request for Windows, at which point its only job is to `Send` a message.

 The WinRT platform is new, so expect it to change and design your application so that you can easily modify it to use new features.

These goals allow me to set a standard for quality and functionality that can be used when testing the app. The remainder of the chapter will focus on the actual application: designing the interface, structuring the pages, and core functionality.

Design of the User Interface

In order to accomplish the goals laid out in this chapter, the Bing Image Search app needs to be small and easy to navigate. With that in mind, the app is broken up into three pages:

- `SearchHistoryPage`

- SearchResultsPage
- DetailsPage

The primary page that the user sees is the SearchHistoryPage; this outlines the user's searching history and is the home screen for the application. Once a user has performed a search, she is navigated to a SearchResultsPage. The SearchResultsPage provides multiple views of the images. There are buttons on the bottom of the app bar that allow users to switch between views. Once an image is selected, the user has the ability to load a DetailsPage where she can perform a number of Windows 8 tasks. Figure 3-2 shows a detailed diagram of the navigation events in the Bing Image Search app.

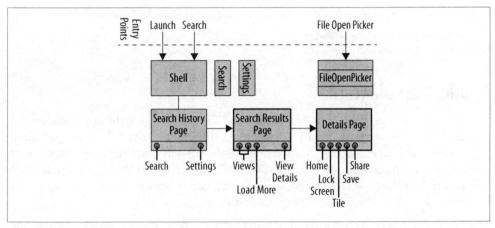

Figure 3-2. Navigation Diagram of Bing Image Search App

Table 3-1. Application Entry Points

Entry Point Override in App.xaml	Description	Bing Image Search app behavior
OnLaunching	Occurs when the user clicks on the tile from the Start Screen or Apps list	Loads the main Shell and navigates to the SearchHistoryPage
OnSearchActivated	Occurs when the user clicks the app icon from within the Windows SearchPane when the app is not currently in the foreground. (i.e., from within another app or from the Start Screen)	Loads the main shell and immediately sends a SearchQueryRequested Message to the MessageHub, which in turn navigates to the SearchRe sultsPage
OnFileOpenPickerActivated	Occurs when the user launches the Fil eOpenPicker from another applica-tion, clicks the Files button, and selects the Bing Image Search app	Loads the custom FileOpenPicker Page and disables navigation

In addition to the overall design of the application, Figure 3-2 also shows the different entry points into the app. All of these entry points, described in Table 3-1, occur in the *App.xaml.cs* file. This *App.xaml* file contains the resource, or style, definitions for use throughout the application. The associated *App.xaml.cs* file contains the `App` class, which, like WPF and Silverlight, hosts the application startup and shutdown event or overrides. This `App` class, or application class, creates a new `Shell` control, assigns it to the current window, and activates that window, as seen in Example 3-1. This main application `Shell` is responsible for the navigation, title, back button, and the `Prefer encesPage`. In the case of the `OnFileOpenPickerActivated` entry point, the full application UI won't suffice for a number of reasons, primarily because the resolution is different and the app bar will not work. This is why it loads a custom page, specifically the `FileOpenPickerPage`, to run the application. The file picker will be described in more detail in Chapter 4.

Example 3-1. A snippet of code used to activate the application Shell (App.xaml.cs)

```
Window.Current.Content = new Shell();
Window.Current.Activate();
```

Application Diagram

The Bing Image Search app is made of Models, Views, ViewModels, application services, and Windows services. Figure 3-3 describes the structure of the Bing Image Search application. This diagram is simplified in a number of ways, but the core components in the application services layer remain. You will also notice that the ViewModels don't talk to the Windows services directly. The application services act as a proxy to the Windows services, which maintains code testability.

The application services are broken up into five categories and I'll review them in the order in which they occur when the application activates:

- MVVM & the ViewModelLocator
- IoC
- NavigationService
- MessagingHub
- ApplicationSettings

Model-View-ViewModel (MVVM)

Model-View-ViewModel (MVVM) is a common practice in XAML and C# that was made popular by WPF and Silverlight. MVVM makes extensive use of the data binding capabilities in XAML. The ViewModel exposes properties on the Model objects *to the* View, which uses data binding to display that information to the user. In addition to binding data from the ViewModel to the View, events from the View are routed to the ViewModel via commands.

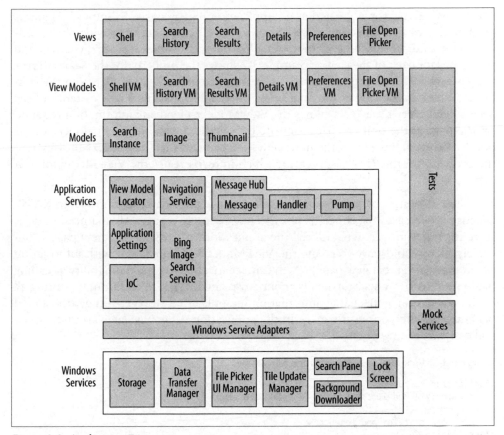

Figure 3-3. Application Diagram

MVVM as a design pattern is a broad topic that I will not be able to cover in this short guide. This section will focus on what's relevant for this app. If you are new to MVVM, you may want to take a look at *WPF Apps With The Model-View-ViewModel Design Pattern*, an article by Josh Smith in MSDN Magazine (*http://msdn.microsoft.com/en-us/maga zine/dd419663.aspx*).

Who Comes First: the View or the ViewModel (the ViewModelLocator)?

There are many schools of thought regarding which object should be created first, the View or the ViewModel. While there are merits in both, I find that using a `ViewModel Locator` for small task-oriented projects, like those typically found in apps for phones and tablets, is easy to manage. This approach may not be appropriate for larger applications because the statically typed nature of the properties may become difficult to manage.

The `ViewModelLocator` is created as an application resource (see Example 3-2) and is used, in this case, with an Inversion of Control (IoC) container to provide object activation for almost everything in the system. Within the `ViewModelLocator`, you will find properties for each of the views. Example 3-3 shows the property for the `SearchHistoryPageViewModel`. This property retrieves an instance of the ViewModel from the container, which in the case of the Bing Image Search app, returns a new instance of the ViewModel every time. This allows the ViewModel to load any information required for the page at the time the page is created. Example 3-4 shows the final piece of the puzzle. When a new page—the new View—loads, it sets its `DataContext` in XAML to the property on the `ViewModelLocator`, which in turn creates the ViewModel for that page.

The View-first style of MVVM works well with the page navigation model in XAML because it decreases the concerns prior to navigating to a page. All you need to do is store the current user state and tell the application to navigate to a new page. Conversely, you would have to create the ViewModel and populate it with information before navigating to a new page, which can negatively affect maintainability as calling pages need to know specific details about any related pages. In addition, by storing all of the navigation state change information in application storage, you get the added benefit of saving your user's place in the application as he navigates around, which makes tombstoning easier.

Example 3-2. ViewModelLocator creation (App.xaml)

```
<Application.Resources>
    <common:ViewModelLocator x:Key="ViewModelLocator" />

    <!-- Other styles and resources --->
</Application.Resources>
```

Example 3-3. SearchHistoryPageViewModel Property in the ViewModelLocator (ViewModelLocator.cs)

```
public SearchHistoryPageViewModel SearchHistoryPageViewModel
{
    get { return Container.Resolve<SearchHistoryPageViewModel>(); }
}
```

Example 3-4. SearchHistoryPage DataContext Binding to ViewModel (SearchHistoryPage.xaml)

```
<Page x:Class="BingImageSearch.SearchHistoryPage"
    xmlns="http://schemas.microsoft.com/winfx/2006/xaml/presentation"
    xmlns:x="http://schemas.microsoft.com/winfx/2006/xaml"
    DataContext="{Binding SearchHistoryPageViewModel,
            Source={StaticResource ViewModelLocator}}">
    <!-- code removed for clarity -->
</Page>
```

Commands

Instead of handling events in the code-behind, which is difficult to test, the MVVM pattern leverages commands to respond to user interactivity. A command is nothing more than a generic interface in WinRT. The way I've chosen to implement them uses a `DelegateCommand`, which can be found in numerous places including the Prism Framework for WPF and Silverlight. Once you've included the `DelegateCommand`, wiring them up to execute methods is as simple as supplying a delegate to the constructor as seen in Example 3-5. In general, I try to ensure that the ViewModels have minimal responsibilities, except for coordinating with the view. For this reason, many command handlers have a simple action that sends the required message to the `MessageHub` for processing.

 Prism (*http://compositewpf.codeplex.com/*) is a set of guidelines produced by Microsoft's Patterns and Practices team on building applications in WPF. While it's a great example of building full-scale applications, I find the techniques described in the Windows Phone 7 Guide to be far more relevant to Windows 8 apps (*http://wp7guide.codeplex .com/*).

Example 3-5. Defining a Command (SearchHistoryPageViewModel.cs)

```csharp
public SearchHistoryPageViewModel(/*  insert dependencies here */)
{
    // ViewModel setup code
    SearchCommand = new DelegateCommand(Search);
}

public void Search()
{
    // Send a message to the MessageHub.
}
```

Inversion of Control (IoC) Container

Numerous Inversion of Control (IoC) containers have been created by the .NET community and make the process of configuring types for your application quite easy. When leveraging the Dependency Inversion principle (or Dependency Injection) your services will likely have nested dependencies, which lead to quite a bit of setup. The IoC container solves this by handling the setup of your application type mappings in a centralized location. In addition, the IoC container is responsible for maintaining the lifetime of each object in your application. If you want more info about IoC containers, there is plenty of information online. My favorite resource is still the DNR TV video *James Kovacs' roll-your-own IoC container* at *http://www.dnrtv.com/default.aspx?show Num=126.*

You should consider carefully which objects you should reuse and which objects you should instantiate on demand, also known as `Single tonLifetime` and `TransientLifetime` respectively. Reusing objects can improve the application's performance at the expense of memory utilization.

Since the .NET Windows 8 App Profile is new, the options for containers are limited. I'd imagine that many more containers will become available with time. For now, I am using a nice container that is available from codeplex called MetroIoC (*http://metroioc .codeplex.com/*).

The `ViewModelLocator` maintains a reference to the application's only IoC container and uses it to create all the ViewModels. Example 3-6 shows how the container is created in the `ViewModelLocator`. It uses a `Lazy<T>` object that builds the container the first time it's requested. The constructor for the lazy object takes a delegate to create an object of the requested type. In the case of Example 3-6, the lazy construction is offloaded to the `IoC.BuildContainer` method, which can be seen in Example 3-7.

Example 3-6. Container declaration (ViewModelLocator.cs)

```
private Lazy<IContainer> _container;
public IContainer Container
{
        get { return _container.Value; }
}

public ViewModelLocator()
{
        _container = new Lazy<IContainer>(IoC.BuildContainer);
}
```

Example 3-7. BuildContainer method (IoC.cs)

```
public class IoC
{
        public static IContainer BuildContainer()
        {
                var container = new MetroContainer();
                container.RegisterInstance(container);
                container.RegisterInstance<IContainer>(container);

                container.Register<IHub, MessageHub>(lifetime: new SingletonLifetime());
                /* more type registrations */
        }
}
```

Once the container is set up, the app is free to use the Dependency Inversion principle throughout. When you look at the `SearchHistoryPageViewModel` class (Example 3-8), you see that the only way to create the object is by supplying two required dependencies in the constructor. The container will automatically determine the requirements and perform the necessary steps to resolve them first and ensure that these requirements are satisfied so that a newly created SearchHistoryPageViewModel can be provided.

Example 3-8. SearchHistoryPageViewModel with dependencies (SearchHistoryPageViewModel.cs)

```
public class SearchHistoryPageViewModel : BindableBase
{
        private readonly INavigationService _navigationService;
        private readonly IHub _hub;

        public SearchHistoryPageViewModel(INavigationService navigationService, IHub hub)
        {
                _navigationService = navigationService;
                _hub = hub;
        }
}
```

 When you couple this design with a unit test, you'll quickly see how much easier this makes your test logic. In the case of the view models, the NavigationService and MessageHub can be mocked and assertions can easily be made on these objects to ensure the proper message is sent when the SearchCommand is executed.

There are numerous benefits to unit testing your code. I will not be covering testing in the book, but the Bing Image Search application has been built with unit tests. If you are interested in my approach to testing, you can find it online at *https://github.com/bendewey/GettingStarted WithMetroApps*.

Navigation

The Bing Image Search app is small, but regardless of your app size, you'll probably need to handle local navigation. There are two main ways to do this: first is to change the Window.Current property to a new UserControl and allow changes in navigation to update that property. The second uses a Frame, which can be set to a Type reference, typically using the typeof keyword, for the XAML page you'd like to display. Both of these approaches have a place, but for the Bing Image Search app, I am going to use the Frame control (Example 3-9). The Frame control works best because it has built-in support for navigation, both forward and backward, and because it allows me to treat the container page (the Shell) as a form of master page or master layout where I can place common UI elements across all pages.

Example 3-9. Frame declaration (Shell.xaml)

```
<Frame x:Name="MainFrame" />
```

This Frame is located in the *Shell.xaml* file. The purpose of the Shell, and the reason I am using a Frame, can be seen in Figure 3-4. The Bing Image Search app will use a

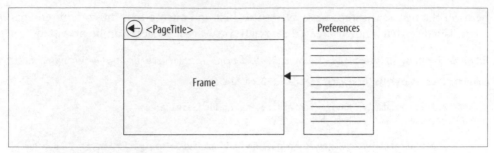

Figure 3-4. Shell sketch with frame marker

consistent title and back button across all pages. The `Shell` will also be used for the preferences page, which will be available from any page.

In order to tell your app to use the *Shell.xaml* file as its default page, you'll need to specify this in the `OnLaunching` event of the *App.xaml.cs* file. Example 3-10 shows what's required to initialize your `Shell` page. In addition to creating the new control and assigning it to the `Window`, the `OnLaunching` event registers the frame with the `ViewModel Locator`'s `NavigationService`. If you remember, the `ViewModelLocator` holds the only container, and the properties on it simply return whatever the container provides, in this case, a `SingletonLifetime` instance of the `NavigationService`.

Example 3-10. Shell initialization (App.xaml.cs)

```
shell = new Shell();
ViewModelLocator.NavigationService.InitializeFrame(shell.Frame);
Window.Current.Content = shell;
Window.Current.Activate();
```

While this code works well for the `OnLaunched` event, the same logic will be needed on the `OnSearchActivated` method. In order to reuse the code between the different activation models, extract this code into a new method and call this from either activation method as in Example 3-11.

Example 3-11. App activation (App.xaml.cs)

```
public override void OnLaunched(/* ... */)
{
        await EnsureShell(args.PreviousExecutionState);
        ViewModelLocator.NavigationService.Navigate(typeof(SearchHistoryPage));
}

public override void OnSearchActivated(/* ... */)
{
        await EnsureShell(args.PreviousExecutionState);
        await ViewModelLocator.Hub.Send(new SearchQuerySubmittedMessage(args.QueryText));
}

public void EnsureShell()
{
```

```
        // setup shell and activate window
}
```

NavigationService

In Example 3-10, I registered the frame with the NavigationService. This service is used throughout the application to handle navigation requests. Example 3-12 shows the NavigationService class, which is essentially a proxy to the Frame methods.

Example 3-12. Using the NavigationService requires a Frame to be initialized (NavigationService.cs)

```
public class NavigationService : INavigationService
{
        private Frame _frame;

        public void InitializeFrame(Frame frame)
        {
                if (_frame != null)
                {
                        _frame.Navigating -= Frame_Navigating;
                }

                _frame = frame;
                _frame.Navigating += Frame_Navigating;
        }

        public void Navigate(Type source, object parameter = null)
        {
                if (_frame == null)
                {
                    throw new InvalidOperationException("Frame has not been initialized.");
                }
                _frame.Navigate(source, parameter);
        }

        /* more proxy methods, CanGoBack, GoBack */
}
```

Once the NavigationService has been initialized, any service can inject it to navigate the application to a new page by calling its navigate method. Example 3-13 shows an example of how the SearchQuerySubmittedHandler handles navigation.

Example 3-13. Using the NavigationService (SearchQuerySubmittedHandler.cs)

```
public class SearchQuerySubmittedHandler : IHandler<SearchQuerySubmittedMessage>
{
        private readonly INavigationService _navigationService;

        public SearchQuerySubmittedHandler(INavigationService navigationService)
        {
                _navigationService = navigationService;
        }

        public void Handle(SearchQuerySubmittedMessage message)
```

```
        {
                // execute the search against the Bing Search API
                _navigationService.Navigate(typeof(SearchResultsPage));
        }
}
```

MessageHub

One of the goals for the Bing Image Search app is to handle application and operate system-level events in a centralized location. To accomplish this, I've implemented a MessageHub, which routes all messages to dedicated handlers that are created by the container, and thus can have their dependencies injected. The MessageHub is made up of four components described in Table 3-2.

Table 3-2. MessageHub Components

Name	Description
MessageHub (IHub)	The MessageHub is the brains behind the operation. It is responsible for receiving the messages and routing them to the appropriate handler.
Message (IMessage)	A Message represents an action in the system. It can signify a user interaction or a message propagated from an operating system event. Messages can have properties in order to notify the handler of information relevant to that event. In the example of a SearchQuerySubmittedMessage, the message would contain the search text entered by the user.
Handler (IHandler and IAsyncHandler)	A handler requires a single method called Handle or HandleAsync, which takes an IMessage as its only parameter. The difference between IHandler and IAsyncHandler is the return type. The async version returns a new Task so it can be awaited. Handlers are constructed using the same IoC container that builds the ViewModels as seen previously in this chapter. If you're interested in how to handle specific Windows 8 tasks, the handlers section is a great place to start.
MessagePump (IMessagePump)	Certain messages are not triggered by user interaction, but by Windows 8. Rather than take dependencies on events throughout the code, message pumps provide a mechanism to listen to system events and pump them out to the MessageHub when they occur. IMessagePump has Start() and Stop() methods, which are used to subscribe and unsubscribe to event handlers, respectively.

Sending a Message

The MessageHub will be used throughout Chapter 4, so in order to get familiar with how it works, I'll show you an end-to-end example. In the previous section I used a Search QuerySubmittedMessage to demonstrate navigation and dependency injection. When the application launches with a search command from Windows (OnSearchActivated), the application class sends a new SearchQuerySubmittedMessage with the search text to the MessageHub. The MessageHub (Example 3-15) locates a handler for the new message and calls the Handle method. The final step is for the handler to receive the message and process it Example 3-16.

Example 3-14. OnSearchActivated (App.xaml.cs)

```
protected override async void OnSearchActivated(SearchActivatedEventArgs args)
{
        await EnsureShell(args.PreviousExecutionState);
        await ViewModelLocator.Hub.Send(new SearchQuerySubmittedMessage(args.QueryText));
}
```

Example 3-15. MessageHub class for routing all messages in the app (MessageHub.cs)

```
public class MessageHub : IHub
{
        private readonly IContainer _container;

        public MessageHub(IContainer container)
        {
                _container = container;
        }

        public async Task Send<TMessage>(TMessage message) where TMessage : IMessage
        {
                var handler = _container.TryResolve<IHandler<TMessage>>(null);
                if (handler != null)
                {
                        handler.Handle(message);
                        return;
                }

                var asyncHandler = _container.TryResolve<IAsyncHandler<TMessage>>(null);
                if (asyncHandler != null)
                {
                        await asyncHandler.HandleAsync(message);
                        return;
                }
        }
}
```

Example 3-16. The message handler for the SearchQuerySubmittedMessage (SearchQuerySubmittedHandler.cs)

```
public class SearchQuerySubmittedHandler : IAsyncHandler<SearchQuerySubmittedMessage>
{
    public SearchQuerySubmittedHandler(/* dependencies */)
```

```
    {
    }

    public async Task HandleAsync(SearchQuerySubmittedMessage message)
    {
        // execute search using message.Query
    }
}
```

Alternatives to the MessageHub

Prism uses a similar pattern called the EventAggregator. This approach allows for multiple handlers, known as subscribers, to listen for notification when an event is sent or published. This approach allows for more flexibility in the handling of events, at the expense of extra setup on the side of the subscribing classes.

Application Storage and Tombstoning

The new application model for Windows 8 apps will suspend your app shortly after your app leaves the user's foreground. It's up to the app to handle reloading to the correct location and retaining the state of the application when the user was last active. This process is known as *tombstoning* your application and is common practice on phones and tablet devices. One approach to handling this is to save your application state when the OnSuspending event occurs in the *App.xaml.cs* file. An alternative approach—and the approach that is used by the Bing Image Search app—is to constantly save state while the user navigates through the application. The latter allows us to use the same tracking mechanism to pass state between different objects in the system.

To accomplish this, the Bing Image Search app uses an ApplicationSettings class. This class is a strongly typed wrapper over the internal ISuspensionManager that maintains the settings in a Dictionary of key-value pairs and contains two methods: SaveAsync and RestoreAsync.

Example 3-17 shows how the SearchResultsPageViewModel updates the Application Settings with the currently selected image and then navigates to the DetailsPage, which loads the selected image from the same application settings location.

Example 3-17. Snippet for setting current image in application settings (SearchResultsPageViewModel.cs)

```
public class SearchResultsPageViewModel : BindableBase
{
        private readonly ApplicationSettings _settings;
        private readonly INavigationService _navigationService;

        public SearchResultsPageViewModel(ApplicationSettings settings,
                INavigationService navigationService)
        {
                _settings = settings;
```

```
        _navigationService = navigationService;

        // Additional ViewModel setup code
        ViewDetailsCommand = new DelegateCommand(ViewDetails);
    }

    public ImageResult SelectedImage
    {
        get { return _settings.SelectedImage;  }
        set
        {
            _settings.SelectedImage = value;
            OnPropertyChanged();
        }
    }

    public void ViewDetails()
    {
        _navigationService.Navigate(typeof(DetailsPage));
    }
}
```

Now that all the settings and other relevant information about the state within the application have been saved, the only remaining concern is reloading the data for the user's return to the app. Example 3-18 shows how, with a simple modification to the EnsureShell method, you can restore the application state.

 Windows 8 apps are not required to save and restore state every time the application relaunches. Depending on your application requirements, you should reserve saving and restoring large objects and files for when the app launches after being terminated. To determine this, you can check the ApplicationExecutionState on the OnLaunching method for Terminated or ClosedByUser. More information about the application lifecycle can be found online at *http://msdn.microsoft.com/ en-us/library/windows/apps/hh464925.aspx*.

Example 3-18. Restoring application settings (App.xaml.cs)

```
public async void EnsureShell()
{
    if (previousState == ApplicationExecutionState.Terminated
        || previousState == ApplicationExecutionState.ClosedByUser)
    {
        var settings = ViewModelLocator.Container.Resolve<ApplicationSettings>();
        await settings.RestoreAsync();
    }

    // Remaining EnsureShell logic from earlier
}
```

Settings

One of the charms on the new Windows 8 Start Bar is the Settings charm. This mechanism is consistent across all apps for providing settings to the user. In the case of the Bing Image Search app, there is only one settings page called Preferences. The preferences UI exists in a UserControl that is located in the main `Shell` (see Example 3-19). By default, the `PreferencesPage` is hidden. In order to display the `Preferences Page`, you need to register a setting as a `SettingsCommand` and provide a callback to show the page. Example 3-20 shows the registration command and the callback.

Example 3-19. Preference page in Shell (Shell.xaml)

```
<UserControl x:Class="BingImageSearch.Shell"
    xmlns="http://schemas.microsoft.com/winfx/2006/xaml/presentation"
    xmlns:x="http://schemas.microsoft.com/winfx/2006/xaml"
        xmlns:local="using:BingImageSearch"
        Loaded="UserControl_Loaded">

        <Grid x:Name="LayoutRoot">
                <!-- Some code removed for clarity -->

                <local:PreferencesPage x:Name="PreferencesPage" Grid.RowSpan="2" />
        </Grid>
</UserControl>
```

Example 3-20. Settings command registration (Shell.xaml.cs)

```
private void RegisterSettings()
{
        SettingsPane.GetForCurrentView().CommandsRequested += (s, e) =>
        {
            var settingsCommand = new SettingsCommand("Preferences", "Preferences", (h) =>
                {
                        this.PreferencesPage.Show();
                });

                e.Request.ApplicationCommands.Add(settingsCommand);
        };
}
```

While the `ApplicationSettings` class stores settings for application state, it is also used to store the user settings for the application. The `PreferencesViewModel`, Example 3-21 uses the same `ApplicationSettings` class to instantly store any changes made by the user. You can see this by the call to `_settings.Rating = value` after calling the base class `SetProperty` method. When the user closes the settings view, these changes are immediately available for use within the app.

Example 3-21. Preferences are saved to settings after updating the property (PreferencesViewModel.cs)

```
public class PreferencesViewModel : BindableBase
{
```

```csharp
    private readonly ApplicationSettings _settings;

    public PreferencesViewModel(ApplicationSettings settings)
    {
        _settings = settings;
        ImageResultSize = _settings.ImageResultSize;
        Rating = _settings.Rating;
    }

    private ResultSize _imageResultSize;
    public ResultSize ImageResultSize
    {
        get { return _imageResultSize; }
        set
        {
            if (value != ResultSize.Empty)
            {
                base.SetProperty(ref _imageResultSize, value);
                _settings.ImageResultSize = value;
            }
        }
    }

    private Rating _rating;
    public Rating Rating
    {
        get { return _rating; }
        set
        {
            if (value != Rating.Empty)
            {
                base.SetProperty(ref _rating, value);
                _settings.Rating = value;
            }
        }
    }
}
```

Summary

Now that a rough idea of the application architecture, it's time to start hooking into the operating system features. The next chapter focuses on all the powerful features within Windows 8 and how they fit into the application design.

CHAPTER 4

Interacting with the Operating System

One of the many reasons to choose a native app over a web app is to have access to the features available exclusively to native apps. This chapter focuses on these features and what it takes for you to implement them into your app.

Just like the previous chapter, I will be using the Bing Image Search application for context when describing these features. As the name states, search is a critical component to the application and it is where I will start. Once the user has performed a search, the app will have images that can be used throughout the operating system in places like tiles, file pickers, and sharing requests. Table 4-1 shows a list of the features that are leveraged by the Bing Image Search app. All of these features will be described in detail in this chapter.

Table 4-1. Windows 8 Features used by the Bing Image Search app

Features	Description
Search	Search is a charm on the Start Bar that enables searching within any application. Search is activated in different ways depending on whether your app is already running or not.
Tiles	Tiles become Live Tiles when you dynamically send updates to them with relevant content for your application. Tiles can be updated with a variety of templates, in the case of the Bing Image Search application, Tiles can be updated with a single image or a collage of images.
Pickers	Pickers are used throughout Windows to provide information to and from applications and the operating system. The Bing Image Search app uses the `FileSavePicker` to save images and the `FileOpenPicker` to provide the searched images to other applications.
Share	Apps can act as either sharing sources or targets. The Bing Image Search application will be used as a share source, meaning that it can share images to other applications. This app will not be used as a share target since it has no use for input data from other apps.

Features	Description
Devices	Windows 8 supports a number of devices such as cameras, light sensors, and accelerometers. The Bing Image Search application uses the Accelerometer to determine when the device is shaken so that it can load more results.

Search

In Chapter 2, I used a TextBox and a Button to load results from the Bing Search API. Although this worked, it didn't fit into the Windows 8 experience. Windows 8 has completely redesigned search on the operating system and has exposed a consistent experience for all applications and files alike. Windows 8 Search can communicate with your app in two ways:

Your app is in the foreground and currently running
 Windows 8 fires an event via the SearchPane.QuerySubmitted handler

Your app is not running
 Windows 8 launches your app with the expressed intent of searching and launches via the overridden OnSearchActivated method within your application (App) class.

Declaring Your Search Intentions

In order to display the app's tile in the SearchPane, you need to specify your intentions via the application manifest file (Package.appxmanifest). This manifest file is located in the root folder of your app and Visual Studio will open a custom screen for defining your app when you open it. Navigate to the Declarations tab, Figure 4-1, select Search from the drop-down menu, and click Add. In the case of the Bing Image Search app, I did not need to specify any parameters because the search logic is handled by the default App entry point. In the event that your app needs an alternative entry point for searching, you could specify it here.

Handling SearchPane.QuerySubmitted

SearchPane.QuerySubmitted is an event on a statically accessible object triggered by the operating system. This type of object is not testable because you don't know when or how the operating system will fire the event. More importantly, you are unable to trigger the event from an automated test. In order to make these events more testable, they need to be converted into messages and routed through the messaging system. When the app runs, the message is sent directly to the handler that performs the actual search. To test the handler, you can easily create a fake message and execute the handler with that message. The mechanism for converting the operating system events into messages that can be handled is the SearchPaneMessagePump (Example 4-1). In addition, this pump

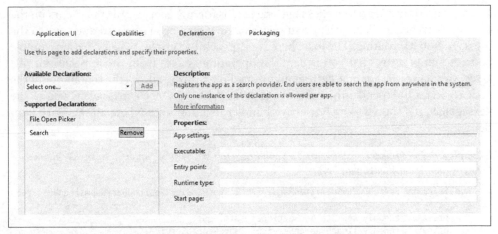

Figure 4-1. Declaring search

can be started when the application launches and can respond to search requests from the operating system regardless of the current page.

Example 4-1. MessagePump adapter to route Windows 8 Searches to the app (SearchPaneMessagePump.cs)

```csharp
public class SearchPaneMessagePump : IMessagePump
{
    private readonly IHub _messageHub;
    private SearchPane _searchPane;

    public SearchPaneMessagePump(IHub messageHub)
    {
        _messageHub = messageHub;
    }

    public void Start()
    {
        _searchPane = SearchPane.GetForCurrentView();
        _searchPane.QuerySubmitted += OnQuerySubmitted;
    }

    public void Stop()
    {
        if (_searchPane != null)
        {
            _searchPane.QuerySubmitted -= OnQuerySubmitted;
        }
    }

    private async void OnQuerySubmitted(SearchPane sender,
                            SearchPaneQuerySubmittedEventArgs args)
    {
        await _messageHub.Send(new SearchQuerySubmittedMessage(args.QueryText));
    }
}
```

When started, the SearchPaneMessagePump listens for any QuerySubmitted events on the current SearchPane. When the event occurs a new message is created and sent to the message hub for routing. The logic here is purposefully simple. When creating testable code, it's imperative that you isolate the operating system from the application; this layer, similar to the adapter pattern mentioned previously, allows the remainder of the code to adapt independently from the operating system. Once a message is sent to the MessageHub, it's routed to its respective handler. Handlers are where all the work happens.

Example 4-2. Handler code for responding to a Search query from Windows 8 (SearchQuerySubmittedHandler.cs)

```
public class SearchQuerySubmittedHandler : IAsyncHandler<SearchQuerySubmittedMessage>
{
    private readonly ApplicationSettings _settings;
    private readonly IImageSearchService _imageSearchService;
    private readonly INavigationService _navigationService;
    private readonly IStatusService _statusService;

    public SearchQuerySubmittedHandler(ApplicationSettings settings, IImageSearchService
        imageSearchService, INavigationService navigationService,
        IStatusService statusService)
    {
        _settings = settings;
        _imageSearchService = imageSearchService;
        _navigationService = navigationService;
        _statusService = statusService;
    }

    public async Task HandleAsync(SearchQuerySubmittedMessage message)
    {
        if (!NetworkInterface.GetIsNetworkAvailable())
        {
            _statusService.SetNetworkUnavailable();
            return;
        }

        _statusService.Message = "Loading Images for " + message.Query;
        _statusService.IsLoading = true;

        try
        {
            // Remove any existing searches for this query
            var searches = _settings.Searches;
            var existing = searches.FirstOrDefault(s =>
            s.Query.Equals(message.Query, StringComparison.CurrentCultureIgnoreCase));
            if (existing != null)
            {
                searches.Remove(existing);
            }

            // Search Bing
            var images = await _imageSearchService.Search(message.Query,
```

```
                                  _settings.Rating, _settings.ImageResultSize);
            if (!images.Any())
            {
                _statusService.SetBingUnavailable();
                return;
            }

            // Store results in app settings
            var instance = new SearchInstance()
                            {
                                Images = images,
                                SearchedOn = DateTime.Today,
                                Query = message.Query
                            };
            searches.Insert(0, instance);
            _settings.Searches = searches;
            _settings.SelectedInstance = instance;
            await _settings.SaveAsync();

            // Navigate
            _navigationService.Navigate(typeof(SearchResultsPage));
        }
        catch (InvalidOperationException ex)
        {
            var baseEx = ex.GetBaseException();
            if (baseEx is WebException)
            {
                _statusService.SetBingUnavailable();
                return;
            }
            throw;
        }
        finally
        {
            _statusService.IsLoading = false;
        }
    }
}
```

The `SearchQuerySubmittedHandler` (Example 4-2) performs the following steps:

1. Checks for a valid Internet connection
2. Notifies the application of its status
3. Executes the search against the Bing Search API
4. Stores the results in the settings for retrieval by the ViewModel
5. Navigates to the `SearchResultsPage`

In the event that a user has already searched for an item, it will be removed from the history before proceeding to avoid duplicates. All the logic in the handler is specific to the application and isolated here from any outside influence. In addition, you'll notice that none of the code in this handler is specific to Windows 8. The primary input is a `Message`, which just contains a string containing the search query.

Using the message hub for searching helps provide more testable code. Unfortunately the topic is far too broad and subjective to discuss here in detail. If you're interested in my approach to testing the code, you can see the tests for the SearchQuerySubmittedHandler by viewing them online at *http://github.com/bendewey/GettingStartedWithMetroApps/ blob/master/BingImageSearch/BingImageSearch.Tests/Message/Han dlers/SearchQuerySubmittedHandlerTests.cs.*

One of the goals from Chapter 3 was to ensure an optimal experience when the users are offline. In order to interact with the app, users would first need to perform a search. This means the SearchQuerySubmittedHandler is an ideal place to verify Internet connectivity before executing the web service call. In addition, I am trapping WebExcep tion here and allowing the _statusService to provide a friendly message to the user stating that the application is offline. Figure 4-2 and Figure 4-3 show the messages that are displayed to the user when the app encounters an error performing a search.

Figure 4-2. Network Unavailable message displayed to the user

Figure 4-3. Bing Search API Unavailable message displayed to the user

In the original version of this class, I tried to optimize the code by using an async void method to save the settings in parallel with navigation. This turned out to have numerous issues with regards to my unit tests, but more importantly it caused issues with the handling of exceptions (see the note below for the reasons to avoid the async void method).

An async method has no return type and simply calls an await on some other code that can use `async void RunSomethingAsync()` and `async Task RunSomethingAsync()` interchangeably. Returning a Task allows other code to await on your method, making it appear synchronous, where returning void signifies a fire-and-forget asynchronous block. It's also important to note that using `async void` is an anti-pattern because exceptions thrown from within an `async void` don't currently bubble up to the application unhandled exception handler and the thread is aborted with no notice. I have a post on the Windows Developer forum that references this issue, and hopefully it will be resolved in a future version (*http://social.msdn.microsoft.com/Forums/en-US/winappswithcsharp/thread/bea154b0-08b0-4fdc-be31-058d9f5d1c4e*).

Launching Your App Directly into Search Mode

The second way to interact with the Windows 8 `SearchPane` is through the `OnSearchAc tivated` override method on your application class. This method provides the same information as the `SearchPane.QuerySubmitted`, but it has a different argument called `SearchActivatedEventArgs`. The testability concerns and logic are almost identical to the static event, and luckily the approach from the previous section can be completely reused by simply sending a message to the exact same message hub. Example 4-3 shows the *App.xaml.cs* code needed to send the message.

Example 4-3. OnSearchActivated override (App.xaml.cs)

```
partial class App
{
    public static ViewModelLocator ViewModelLocator
    {
        get { return (ViewModelLocator)Current.Resources["ViewModelLocator"]; }
    }

    protected override async void OnSearchActivated(SearchActivatedEventArgs args)
    {
            await EnsureShell(args.PreviousExecutionState);
            await ViewModelLocator.Hub.Send(new
SearchQuerySubmittedMessage(args.QueryText));
    }

    private async Task EnsureShell(ApplicationExecutionState previousState)
    {
        // setup Container, Shell, and set Window.Current.Content
    }
}
```

There isn't much to expand upon here except for the fact that when the application launches, it loads the UI and sends the same message as the `SearchPaneMessagePump`. Similarly, this message gets routed to the `SearchQuerySubmittedHandler`, which navigates to the SearchResultsPage, except this time it happens immediately upon launching the app.

In addition to these two entry points, applications can provide autocomplete information to the Windows 8 SearchPane. This can help users find information relevant to your content. I can envision an email application that will provide terms present in recent emails as autocomplete hints. This information is also available via events on the SearchPane and would fit nicely into the existing messaging implementation.

Tiles

Tiles are the first view your user will get of your app. From the moment she sees it in the Windows Store to the first time she launches the app, the Tile is your place to make a first impression. Furthermore, once you've engaged your user, it's important to bring her back; Live Tiles offer a way to update users with current information without having to launch the app again.

Tiles come in two sizes: square and wide. Each size has its own set of templates that can be updated independently or as a single update. Templates come in a number of different formats, from simple text updates to multiple images with text. A full list of templates is available online at *http://msdn.microsoft.com/en-us/library/windows/apps/ windows.ui.notifications.tiletemplatetype.aspx*. The Bing Image Search application will utilize three templates listed in Table 4-2.

Table 4-2. TileTemplatesTypes used by the Bing Image Search app

Template	Sample
TileSquarePeekImageAndText04	

Template	Sample
TileWidePeekImage03	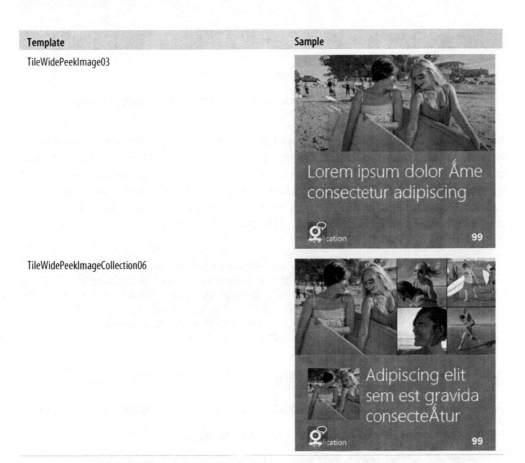
TileWidePeekImageCollection06	

Updating the Tile with a Collection of Images

After performing a search, the user will be navigated to the SearchResults page. This page shows a list of images based on the search. From this list, you can provide your first tile update. The template you choose is entirely up to you; I chose to take a random sampling of six images and update the tile with the `TileWidePeekImageCollection06` template. You'll also need to determine whether you want to update the tile automatically or via some user interaction, for example, when the user clicks on an AppBar button. I chose to update the user's tile automatically when he performs a search. When the `SearchResultsPage` loads, the IoC container creates a new instance of the `SearchResultsPageViewModel`. In the constructor of this view model, and Example 4-4, a message is sent to the message hub to update the tile.

Example 4-4. SearchResultsPageViewModel constructor (SearchResultsPageViewModel.cs)

```
public SearchResultsPageViewModel(ApplicationSettings settings, IHub hub
                                  /* other dependencies */ )
{
```

```
    _settings = settings;
    _hub = hub;

    // setup other depedencies and commands

    _hub.Send(new UpdateTileImageCollectionMessage(_settings.SelectedInstance));
}
```

Sending this message activates the handler, shown in Example 4-5, which is made up of three steps. The first step retrieves the template for the tile. The second updates the content's template with the URLs for the data you would like to update. Finally, the item is sent to the `TileUpdateManagerAdapter` to update the primary live tile. The `TileUpdateManagerAdapter` is an adapter over the static `TileUpdateManager` that is available in the Windows. Example 4-6 shows the `TileUpdateManagerAdapter`.

 The code in Example 4-5 uses NotificationExtensions, a project that was provided by Microsoft as part of their *App tile and badges sample*, which can be found at *http://code.msdn.microsoft.com/windowsapps/ App-tiles-and-badges-sample-5fc49148*. The default API for updating tiles uses a `TileUpdateManager.GetTemplate(type)` to return an `XmlDocu` ment for the template, which can be updated manually.

Example 4-5. Handler code for setting a collection of images to your app tile (UpdateTileImageCollectionHandler.cs)

```
public class UpdateTileImageCollectionHandler : IHandler<UpdateTileImageCollectionMessage>
{
    private readonly ITileUpdateManager _tileUpdateManager;

    public UpdateTileImageCollectionHandler(ITileUpdateManager tileUpdateManager)
    {
        _tileUpdateManager = tileUpdateManager;
    }

    public void Handle(UpdateTileImageCollectionMessage message)
    {
        var content = TileContentFactory.CreateTileWidePeekImageCollection06();

        content.RequireSquareContent = false;
        content.TextHeadingWrap.Text = "Search for " + message.Instance.Query;

        var images = message.Instance.GetRandomImages(6).ToList();
        UpdateImage(content.ImageMain, images[0]);
        UpdateImage(content.ImageSecondary, images[1]);
        UpdateImage(content.ImageSmallColumn1Row1, images[2]);
        UpdateImage(content.ImageSmallColumn1Row2, images[3]);
        UpdateImage(content.ImageSmallColumn2Row1, images[4]);
        UpdateImage(content.ImageSmallColumn2Row2, images[5]);

        _tileUpdateManager.UpdatePrimaryTile(tile);
    }
```

```
    private void UpdateImage(INotificationContentImage imageContent, ImageDetail image)
    {
        imageContent.Src = image.Thumbnail.Url;
        imageContent.Alt = image.Title;
    }
}
```

Example 4-6. Adapter code to send an update to the Windows8 TileUpdateManager (TileUpdateManagerAdapter.cs)

```
public class TileUpdateManagerAdapter : ITileUpdateManager
{
    public void UpdatePrimaryTile(ITileNotificationContent content)
    {
        var notification = content.CreateNotification();
        TileUpdateManager.CreateTileUpdaterForApplication().Update(notification);
    }
}
```

 The Bing Image Search application provides updates to the tile via publicly accessible (HTTP) URIs. Tiles can also be updated with local content using the ms-appx://<local-path> syntax.

Updating Multiple Tiles with a Single Command

In the previous example of the image collection, I chose not to provide square tile content by assigning the RequireSquareContent to false. The main reason for this is there aren't any square tiles that allow for a collection of images. This means the default square tile will continue to be used. What I'd like to do is allow the user to update the square tile on her own via an AppBar button. When the user selects an image, she is navigated to the DetailsPage. This page allows users to do a task specific to the image, such as save, share, update tile, etc. (See Figure 4-4). On the AppBar of the Details Page (Example 4-7), there is a button to set the tile. This button links to a command, which can be found on the view model, as seen in Example 4-8.

Figure 4-4. Image Search Options

Example 4-7. Set Tile AppBar Button (DetailsPage.xaml)

```
<Button Command="{Binding SetTileCommand}"
        Style="{StaticResource SetTileAppBarButtonStyle}" />
```

Example 4-8. SetTile Command (DetailsPageViewModel.cs)

```
public class DetailsPageViewModel
{
    // constructor and dependencies omitted
    public ICommand SetTileCommand { get; set; }

    public void SetTile()
    {
        _messageHub.Send(new UpdateTileMessage(_settings.SelectedImage));
    }
}
```

As you've seen in previous examples, the update tile command is handled by a dedicated message handler in response to the message from the ViewModel. This keeps the ViewModel's responsibilities constrained to just communicating between the View. Once the message is sent to the message hub, the hub executes the handler with the message. Example 4-9 shows the UpdateTileHandler, which is responsible for performing the actual tile update against the operating system.

Example 4-9. Message handler for updating the title to a single image (Update TileHandler.cs)

```
public class UpdateTileHandler : IHandler<UpdateTileMessage>
{
    private readonly ITileUpdateManager _tileUpdateManager;

    public UpdateTileHandler(ITileUpdateManager tileUpdateManager)
    {
        _tileUpdateManager = tileUpdateManager;
    }

    public void Handle(UpdateTileMessage message)
    {
        var url = message.Image.MediaUrl;
        if (message.Image.Width > 800 || message.Image.Height > 800)
        {
            // Images > 800px cannot be used as tiles
            url = message.Image.Thumbnail.Url;
        }

        var content = TileContentFactory.CreateTileWidePeekImageAndText01();
        content.TextBodyWrap.Text = message.Image.Title;
        content.Image.Src = url;
        content.Image.Alt = message.Image.Title;

        // Square image substitute
        var squareContent = TileContentFactory.CreateTileSquareImage();
        squareContent.Image.Src = url;
        squareContent.Image.Alt = message.Image.Title;
        content.SquareContent = squareContent;

        _tileUpdateManager.UpdatePrimaryTile(content);
    }
}
```

With the exception of a change in the template, the logic in the single update Tile handler is very similar to the handler for updating a collection of images. I'm retrieving the template, setting its values, and updating the Tile through the `TileUpdateManagerA dapter`. Depending on the size of your images you may have to perform some resizing. Live tiles do not work with images larger than 800 pixels tall or wide. In the case of the Bing Image Search app, this was easy to resolve by verifying the metadata of the image and downgrading it to the thumbnail view in those scenarios.

It's also important to note that in Example 4-9 I am specifying an alternative `Square Content` tile. The content is identical to the wide content and allows the user to change the tile size on the start screen and still receive the tile updates.

Tiles are a great way to make your app stand out. In addition to updating your Live Tile when the app is running, you can also specify a timer or push notification-based background task to update your tiles as well. Background Tasks are declared in the application manifest similar to how search was declared in the previous section. This is a handy way to provide updates to your app's Tile in the event that your app hasn't been launched recently. In addition to providing these images to the Tile, these images can also be provided to other apps directly via pickers.

Pickers

Pickers are used to provide information to and from your app. For example, your app can provide information to the `FileOpenPicker`, in which case other apps can use your content. Conversely, your app can be the one consuming the content from a `FileOpen Picker`, which in turn allows your app to receive content from any installed app on the user's system that is providing information. Typically speaking handling a picker is far more difficult than consuming one. The Bing Image Search app will leverage two of the pickers.

FileOpenPicker
> The Bing Image Search app will support the `FileOpenPicker` for any app that requests image files. This will utilize a custom page that will provide a `TextBox` and a `Button` for searching.

FileSavePicker
> The Bing Image Search app will utilize the `FileSavePicker` from the `DetailsPage` to save an image. This can be used to save a picture to the local filesystem or to save it to another app, like the SkyDrive app, which allows users to save files to the cloud directly through this mechanism.

FileOpenPicker

Declaring the FileOpenPicker in the manifest

Before you can support the `FileOpenPicker`, you must specify your intentions via the application manifest. This will make your application icon appear in the list of available apps when a user launches a `FileOpenPicker`. To specify your declaration, open the `Package.appxmanifest` on the root of your project, and select the Declarations tab. Select File Open Picker from the drop-down list and click Add. In the case of the Bing Image Search app, the `FileOpenPicker` is limited to supplying only image files (see Figure 4-5), but depending on your needs you can specify other types or choose to support any file type by checking the Supports Any File Type checkbox.

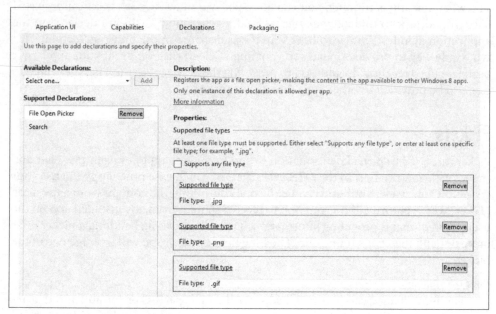

Figure 4-5. Declaring File Open Picker

Launching the FileOpenPicker

Once you've declared your app, you are ready to hook up the entry point. The Bing Image Search application doesn't supply any explicit entry point for the `FileOpen Picker`. In that case, the app will launch the **App** class as its entry point. In the **App** class, there is an `override void OnFileOpenPickerActivated` (Example 4-10), which will execute. The Bing Image Search app will create a custom `FilePickerPage`, rather than the typical **Shell** page, and set the current window's content to that page. In order to handle adding and remove items to/from the picker, you need to use the supplied `FileOpen PickerActivatedEventArgs`, which provides access to the `FileOpenPickerUI`. This is the only time you can access this object, so you'll need to hang on to it. I've created a custom wrapper that is registered in the container and is initialized with the current `FileOpen PickerUI`. This wrapper will also serve as an adapter to allow testability of the `FilePick erPageViewModel`. Example 4-11 and Example 4-12 show the interface and wrapper used for adding and removing items to/from the picker.

Example 4-10. OnFileOpenPickerActivated override (App.xaml.cs)

```
protected override void OnFileOpenPickerActivated(FileOpenPickerActivatedEventArgs args)
{
        ViewModelLocator.FileOpenPickerUiManager.Initialize(args.FileOpenPickerUI);
        Window.Current.Content = new FilePickerPage();
        Window.Current.Activate();
}
```

Example 4-11. IFileOpenPickerUiManager interface (IFileOpenPickerUiManager.cs)

```
public interface IFileOpenPickerUiManager
{
    void Initialize(FileOpenPickerUI fileOpenPicker);

    FileSelectionMode SelectionMode { get; }
    IReadOnlyList<string> AllowedFileTypes { get; }
    AddFileResult AddFile(string id, IStorageFile storageFile);
    void RemoveFile(string id);
}
```

Example 4-12. FileOpenPickerUiManager implementation (FileOpenPickerUiManager.cs)

```
public class FileOpenPickerUiManager : IFileOpenPickerUiManager
{
    private FileOpenPickerUI _fileOpenPicker;

    public void Initialize(FileOpenPickerUI fileOpenPicker)
    {
        _fileOpenPicker = fileOpenPicker;
    }

    public FileSelectionMode SelectionMode
    {
        get { return _fileOpenPicker.SelectionMode; }
    }

    public IReadOnlyList<string> AllowedFileTypes
    {
        get { return _fileOpenPicker.AllowedFileTypes; }
    }

    public AddFileResult AddFile(string id, IStorageFile file)
    {
        return _fileOpenPicker.AddFile(id, file);
    }

    public void RemoveFile(string id)
    {
        _fileOpenPicker.RemoveFile(id);
```

```
    }
}
```

The `FilePickerPage` is similar to the Bing Simple Search app from Chapter 2. This page contains a `TextBox`, a `Button`, and a `GridView` (Example 4-13). Unlike the first example, this page needs to handle adding and removing files from the picker upon user selection. In addition, the page also needs to support multiple selections. Because this is difficult to accomplish with data binding, I resorted to using the code behind and routing custom events to the ViewModel based on the user selection. Example 4-14 shows the code-behind necessary to facilitate the `ItemGridView_SelectionChanged` event handler.

Example 4-13. FilePickerPage XAML (FilePickerPage.xaml)

```xml
<Grid x:Name="LayoutRoot">
    <Grid.RowDefinitions>
        <RowDefinition Height="87" />
        <RowDefinition />
    </Grid.RowDefinitions>
    <Grid VerticalAlignment="Center" Margin="120,0,0,0">
        <Grid.ColumnDefinitions>
            <ColumnDefinition />
            <ColumnDefinition Width="Auto" />
        </Grid.ColumnDefinitions>
        <TextBox Text="{Binding SearchQuery, Mode=TwoWay}" />
        <Button Content="Search" Command="{Binding SearchCommand}"
                            Margin="12,0,60,0" Grid.Column="1" />
    </Grid>
    <Grid x:Name="ItemPickerContentPanel" Grid.Row="1" Margin="120,0,0,34">
        <GridView x:Name="ItemGridView"
            ItemsSource="{Binding Source={StaticResource CollectionViewSource}}"
            ItemTemplate="{StaticResource ThumbnailItemTemplate}"
            ItemContainerStyle="{StaticResource GridTileStyle}"
            BorderThickness="0" VerticalAlignment="Stretch"
            Grid.Row="1"
            SelectionMode="Multiple"
            SelectionChanged="ItemGridView_SelectionChanged" />
    </Grid>
</Grid>
```

Example 4-14. FileOpenPickerPage code behind showing the custom routing needed in lieu of data binding commands (FileOpenPickerPage.xaml.cs)

```csharp
public sealed partial class FileOpenPickerPage
{
    protected FileOpenPickerPageViewModel ViewModel
    {
        get { return DataContext as FileOpenPickerPageViewModel; }
    }

    private void ItemGridView_SelectionChanged(object sender, SelectionChangedEventArgs e)
    {
        var vm = ViewModel;
        if (vm == null) return;
```

```
            foreach(var image in e.AddedItems)
            {
                vm.AddImage(image);
            }
            foreach(var image in e.RemovedItems)
            {
                vm.RemoveImage(image);
            }
        }
    }
}
```

Handling the FileOpenPickerUI

Now that the XAML and page are set up to communicate with the ViewModel, the actual files can be sent to the picker. In addition to searching, the `FileOpenPickerPage` `ViewModel` (Example 4-15) handles adding and removing items to and from the `FileO` `penPickerUiManager` shown earlier. This object is injected by the container into the constructor of the ViewModel, and when an item is added by the page, the ViewModel downloads the item and adds it to the manager.

Example 4-15. ViewModel for the FileOpenPicker page (FileOpenPickerPageViewModel.cs)

```
public class FileOpenPickerPageViewModel : BindableBase
{
    private readonly ApplicationSettings _settings;
    private readonly IFileOpenPickerUiManager _fileOpenPicker;

    public FileOpenPickerPageViewModel(ApplicationSettings settings,
      IFileOpenPickerUiManager fileOpenPicker /* other dependenceies */)
    {
        _settings = settings;
        _fileOpenPicker = fileOpenPicker;
        // ViewModel setup code omitted
    }

    // Search code omitted for clarity

    public async void AddImage(object item)
    {
        var image = item as ImageResult;
        if (image == null) return;

        if (_fileOpenPicker.AllowedFileTypes.Any(ext =>
                    ext == "*" || image.MediaUrl.EndsWith(ext)))
        {
            var file = await _settings.GetTempFileAsync(image.MediaUrl);
            var result = _fileOpenPicker.AddFile(image.MediaUrl, file);
        }
    }

    public void RemoveImage(object item)
    {
        var image = item as ImageResult;
        if (image == null) return;
```

```
    _fileOpenPicker.RemoveFile(image.MediaUrl);
    }
}
```

It's important to note that not all requests can handle the supported file types. Your app is responsible for handling these cases and providing only files that are contained within the AllowedFileTypes list. In the event that you supply an invalid file, you can check the AddFileResult object that is returned from the call to AddFile.

The downloading of the file is an asynchronous method handled by the Application Settings class and shown in Example 4-16. This method uses an extremely useful API, the BackgroundDownloader, this object is used as the primary method for downloading static content. The BackgroundDownloader is extremely easy to use, and with only a few lines of code I am able to download a file and provide it to anything that needs a StorageFile. The actual code for the BackgroundDownloader is accessed via the Back groundDownloadAdapter, which can be found in Example 4-17.

Example 4-16. ApplicationSettings GetTempFileAsync method to download files for the file picker (ApplicationSettings.cs)

```
public async Task<StorageFile> GetTempFileAsync(string uri)
{
    return await CreateAndDownloadFile(uri);
}

private async Task<StorageFile> CreateAndDownloadFile(string uri, string filename = null)
{
    filename = filename ?? Regex.Replace(uri, "https?://|[/?&#]", "");
    StorageFile file = await ApplicationData.Current.LocalFolder.CreateFileAsync(filename,
      CreationCollisionOption.ReplaceExisting);
    await _backgroundDownloader.StartDownloadAsync(new Uri(uri), file);
    return file;
}
```

Example 4-17. BackgroundDownloader Adapter (BackgroundDownloaderAdapter.cs)

```
public class BackgroundDownloaderAdapter : IBackgroundDownloader
{
        public IAsyncOperationWithProgress<DownloadOperation, DownloadOperation>
                        StartDownloadAsync(Uri uri, IStorageFile storageFile)
        {
                return new BackgroundDownloader().CreateDownload(uri, storageFile)
                        .StartAsync();
        }
}
```

Now that the page is successfully adding and removing content to the picker its job is done. Testing the FileOpenPicker can be tricky, though. In Visual Studio, if you run you app, you will launch the app using the standard OnLaunching entry point. To trigger the OnFileOpenPickerActivated entry point, you need to access your app from the FileOpenPicker. Microsoft provides a sample app, which can aid in testing, but I've found that the mail application is a great tool for testing the `FileOpenPicker` (*http://code .msdn.microsoft.com/windowsapps/File-picker-app-extension-0cb95155*). Just launch the mail app, create a new message, and click Add Attachment. This will launch the `FileOpenPicker`.

FileSavePicker

The Bing Image Search application uses the `FileSavePicker` to save an image. Consuming the pickers is far easier than supporting them. All that you need to do is open the dialog with your necessary parameters and handle the response. The beauty is that your app doesn't really care where the `StorageFile` is coming from, just that you can write some data to it. In addition, you don't have to create any declarations, to use a picker you just create one, tell it to pick files, and leverage the results in any app. Example 4-18 shows XAML and Example 4-19 shows the code in the `DetailsPageView Model` that sends the `SaveImageMessage`.

Example 4-18. Save Image AppBar (DetailsPage.xaml)

```
<Button x:Name="SaveCommand"Command="{Binding SaveCommand}"
        Style="{StaticResource SaveAppBarButtonStyle}" />
```

Example 4-19. Save Command (DetailsPageViewModel.cs)

```
public class DetailsPageViewModel
{
    // constructor and dependencies omitted
    public ICommand SaveCommand { get; set; }

    public async Task Save()
    {
        await_messageHub.Send(new SaveImageMessage(_settings.SelectedImage));
    }
}
```

In line with other messages in the system, the `SaveImageMessage` is handled by the corresponding `SaveImageHandler` (Example 4-20). The `SaveImageHandler` is responsible for opening the `FileSavePicker`. However, before it can do this, it needs to create a new `FileSavePicker` object, define the file type filters, and provide a suggested name. In the case of the Bing Image Search app, I am using the actual filename from the URL as the suggested filename. Once the picker is defined, you can call `PickSaveFileAsync`, which will actually prompt the user with a new Windows 8 file save dialog (Figure 4-6). The result of this call will be a `StorageFile` for the selected file, or null if the user clicks Cancel. With that selected file, I can kick off a download from a remote location, which will automatically save directly to the selected file. When the process is complete, I update the `_statusService` for the application.

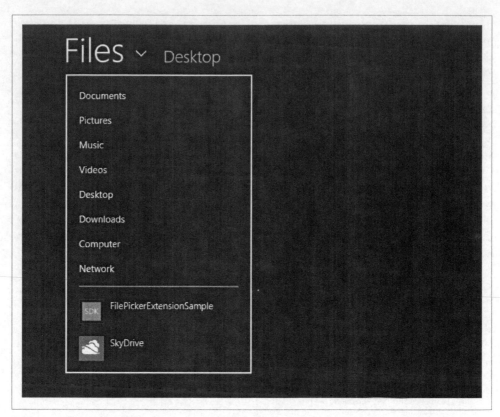

Figure 4-6. File Save Picker

Example 4-20. SaveImageHandler

```
public class SaveImageHandler : IAsyncHandler<SaveImageMessage>
{
    private readonly IPickerFactory _pickerFactory;
    private readonly IBackgroundDownloader _backgroundDownloader;
    private readonly IStatusService _statusService;

    public SaveImageHandler(IPickerFactory pickerFactory,
        IBackgroundDownloader backgroundDownloader,
        IStatusService statusService)
    {
        _pickerFactory = pickerFactory;
        _backgroundDownloader = backgroundDownloader;
        _statusService = statusService;
    }

    public async Task HandleAsync(SaveImageMessage message)
    {
        // Set up and launch the Open Picker
        var filename = GetFilenameFromUrl(message.Image.MediaUrl);
        var extension = System.IO.Path.GetExtension(filename);
```

```
        var picker = _pickerFactory.CreateFileSavePicker();
        picker.SuggestedFileName = filename;
        picker.FileTypeChoices.Add(extension.Trim('.').ToUpper(),
                        new string[] { extension });

        var saveFile = await picker.PickSaveFileAsync();
        if (saveFile != null)
        {
            await _backgroundDownloader.StartDownloadAsync(
                            new Uri(message.Image.MediaUrl), saveFile);

            _statusService.TemporaryMessage =
                string.Format("Image {0} saved.", saveFile.Name);
        }
    }

    private string GetFilenameFromUrl(string url)
    {
        var uri = new System.Uri(url);
        return uri.Segments[uri.Segments.Length - 1];
    }
}
```

In the `SaveImageHandler`, you may have noticed that I didn't create a new `FileSave Picker` in the handler directly. This is not testable for a number of reasons. First off, the `FileSavePicker` launches a new dialog and requires user interaction. This workflow cannot be automated. In addition, just creating a new `FileSavePickerAdapter` in the Handle method wouldn't allow for providing alternative implementations. In order to solve these concerns, I create a `PickerFactory` object, which returns a new `FileSave PickerAdapter` for every request in production. This factory can then be customized by a test to return whatever is needed. The `PickerFactory` and `FileSavePickerAdapter` can be seen in Example 4-21 and Example 4-22, respectively. The `FileSavePickerAdapter` is a bit more in depth than other adapters because it contains properties that need to be mapped as well. It purposefully has no external business logic because this class cannot be tested.

Example 4-21. PickerFactory

```
public class PickerFactory : IPickerFactory
{
        public IFileSavePickerAdapter CreateFileSavePicker()
        {
                return new FileSavePickerAdapter();
        }
}
```

Example 4-22. FileSavePickerAdapter

```
public class FileSavePickerAdapter : IFileSavePickerAdapter
{
        public FileSavePickerAdapter()
        {
                CommitButtonText = String.Empty;
```

```
                FileTypeChoices = new Dictionary<string, IList<string>>();
                SuggestedFileName = String.Empty;
                // The system default is DocumentsLibrary, but this app is all about images
                SuggestedStartLocation = PickerLocationId.PicturesLibrary;
        }

        public string CommitButtonText { get; set; }
        public string DefaultFileExtension { get; set; }
        public IDictionary<string, IList<string>> FileTypeChoices { get; set; }
        public string SuggestedFileName { get; set; }
        public PickerLocationId SuggestedStartLocation { get; set; }

        public async Task<IStorageFile> PickSaveFileAsync()
        {
                var picker = new FileSavePicker();
                picker.CommitButtonText = CommitButtonText;
                picker.SuggestedFileName = SuggestedFileName;
                picker.SuggestedStartLocation = SuggestedStartLocation;
                if (DefaultFileExtension != null)
                {
                        picker.DefaultFileExtension = DefaultFileExtension;
                }

                foreach(var choice in FileTypeChoices.Keys)
                {
                        picker.FileTypeChoices.Add(choice, FileTypeChoices[choice]);
                }

                return await picker.PickSaveFileAsync();
        }
}
```

Pickers are a compelling reason to develop a native app over a web app. Communicating with a user's filesystem is not likely to be included in modern web browsers. Pickers also allow apps to communicate with other applications on the user's machine regardless of the intent and without any knowledge of each other. This is not something that is typically done in Windows, or something that is easily accomplished in any other operating system for that matter.

Sharing

If you have ever written code that communicated with the Windows Clipboard, then sharing should be very familiar. When the user activates the Share charm, an event fires where you can assign text, URIs, data, images, or raw data. On the other end, apps can set up a declaration in their app manifest, which will show the Tile on the share page when the specified type is shared by another application. That target app can then use the content however it sees fit, for example, to send an email.

The Bing Image Search app will act as a sharing source and will provide links and images, also known as bitmap data to other applications. Figure 4-7 shows a screenshot of the sharing pane in action. If the user activates sharing when he is on the search results page, then the app will provide a link to Bing's image search site for that query. If he selects an image and navigates to the details page, then the app will provide the bitmap data for the selected image.

Figure 4-7. Bing Image Search with Sharing

ShareDataRequestedMessagePump

When the user opens the Sharing pane, the `DataTransferManager.DataRequested` event fires. This is very similar to Search from earlier in this chapter, so I followed the same pattern. The event is handled by an application-level message pump. The message pump's job is to convert system events into application messages and route them through the message hub. Unlike the message pump from Search, which acted on information from the event, sharing requires some information be provided to the event. Example 4-23 shows a simplified comparison. Notice how only the DataRequested—Sharing—event requires some content, in this case a string called `"MyAppContent"`.

Example 4-23. Windows 8 Event Differences

```
// event registration code omitted

private void OnQuerySubmitted(SearchPane sender,
                                    SearchPaneQuerySubmittedEventArgs args)
{
        // use args.QueryText to search
}

private void OnDataRequested(DataRequestManager sender,
```

```
                        DataRequestManagerArgs args)
{
        // use args.Request.SetText("MyAppContent") or equivalent.
}
```

Since the app will be sending different types of content, the event handler will send out one of two messages:

ShareUriMessage
> Sharing from the search results page will provide a Uri. The handler will just supply the Uri directly.

ShareImageDetailsMessage
> Sharing from the details page will provide an object of type ImageResult. The handler will download the image and provide the data from there.

These messages are sent based on the ShareDataRequestedMessagePump.DataToShare property, which any page can supply. The current data to share will always be set to the last item specified. Example 4-24 shows how the ShareDataRequestedMessagePump creates a message based on the DataToShare. Another thing to note, is that unlike the search message pump, the share message pump registers its event on an adapter. The reason for this extra level of abstraction is because this message pump isn't as simple as the one for search, so there are areas that I want to test. In addition to test the handlers, we need to have access to create mocks of the DataRequestedEventArgs so that we can ensure that the handlers are working. To do this, the DataTransferManagerAdapter implements the IDataTransferManager interface and wraps the event args in a new SettableDataRequestedEventArgs, which is supplied to the message. Now the handler test can create a test message with a fake event args.

Example 4-24. ShareDataRequestedPump(ShareDataRequestedPump.cs)

```
public class ShareDataRequestedPump : IShareDataRequestedPump
{
    private readonly IDataTransferManager _dataTransferManager;
    private readonly IHub _hub;

    public ShareDataRequestedPump(IDataTransferManager dataTransferManager, IHub hub)
    {
        _dataTransferManager = dataTransferManager;
        _hub = hub;
    }

    public void Start()
    {
        _dataTransferManager.DataRequested += OnDataRequested;
    }

    public void Stop()
    {
        _dataTransferManager.DataRequested -= OnDataRequested;
    }
```

```
public object DataToShare { get; set; }

void OnDataRequested(DataTransferManager sender, SettableDataRequestedEventArgs args)
{
    if (DataToShare == null) return;

    if (DataToShare is Uri)
    {
        var message = new ShareUriMessage((Uri)DataToShare, sender, args);
        _hub.Send(message);
        return;
    }

    if (DataToShare is ImageResult)
    {
        var message = new ShareImageResultsMessage((ImageResult)DataToShare,
            sender, args);
        _hub.Send(message);
        return;
    }
}
}
```

ShareUriHandler

Each of these messages has a dedicated handler. The ShareUriHandler is the easiest, so
I will start with that. The ShareUriHandler handles the ShareUriMessage. This message
contains the data to share—in this case, the URI to share—and the event args, which
I will use to set the URI on. Example 4-25 shows the ShareUriHandler and the code
needed to respond to the message. This code is fairly straightforward. When the message is received, the handler sets the Title and the URI for the specified data and its job
is done.

Example 4-25. ShareUriHandler

```
public class ShareUriHandler : IHandler<ShareUriMessage>
{
    public void Handle(ShareUriMessage message)
    {
        var request = message.DataRequestedEventArgs.Request;

        request.Data.Properties.Title = "Bing Image Search Link";
        request.Data.SetUri(message.Link);
    }
}
```

ShareImageResultsHandler

When the Bing Image Search app shares images, more specifically images from the
Web, these images need to be downloaded before they can be shared. This becomes

slightly complicated because downloading the image data to provide a stream is an asynchronous process.

The new async and await keywords make the code very simple from a readability standpoint, but the code still executes the way it always has. The reason this is important is because DataRequestManager is expecting the user to set some shareable content before the completion of the event. Example 4-26 shows a very rough translation of what I'm trying to say. The OnDataRequestedWithoutAsync handler sets the data on the event in the second phase of the operation, which is inside a lambda expression. The event handler has already returned control to the caller without anything being set. The way to get around this is to use a new feature in the Windows Runtime called a Deferral. OnDataRequestedWithDeferral. Example 4-26 shows an example of a Deferral.

Example 4-26. Example of why deferrals are needed with async code

```
// BAD: This code will not work because of the await
private async void OnDataRequested(DataRequestManager sender,
                                   DataRequestManagerArgs args)
{
        // code before await
        var file = await DownloadFile();
        // code after await
        args.Request.SetBitmap(file);
        // event handler returned to caller
}

// BAD: This code will not work because event handler returns prematurely
private void OnDataRequestedWithoutAsync(DataRequestManager sender,
                                         DataRequestManagerArgs args)
{
        // code before await
        DownloadFile().ContinueWith(file =>
        {
                // code after await
                args.Request.SetBitmap(file);
        });
        // event handler returned to caller
}

private void OnDataRequestedWithDeferral(DataRequestManager sender,
                                         DataRequestManagerArgs args)
{
        var deferral = args.Request.GetDeferral();
        try
        {
                // code before await
                var file = await DownloadFile();
                // code after await
                args.Request.SetBitmap(file);
        }
        finally
        {
                deferral.Complete();
```

```
        }
        // event handler returned to caller
}

private async Task<IStorageFile> DownloadFile() {}
```

Example 4-27 shows the full ShareImageDetailsHandler. This handler sets the title and the description of the data being shared. It also defines a callback to lazily load the share image when the caller needs it. This will potentially save the user from downloading the image if he prematurely exits out of the Sharing pane. Inside the callback, the handler downloads the image and applies it using the deferral pattern.

Example 4-27. Handler code for sharing and image (ShareImageResultsHandler.cs)

```
public class ShareImageResultsHandler : IHandler<ShareImageResultsMessage>
{
    private readonly ApplicationSettings _settings;

    public ShareImageResultsHandler(ApplicationSettings settings)
    {
        _settings = settings;
    }

    public void Handle(ShareImageResultsMessage message)
    {
        var image = message.Image;
        if (image.MediaUrl != null)
        {
            var request = message.DataRequestedEventArgs.Request;
            request.Data.Properties.Title = "Bing Search Image";
            request.Data.Properties.Description =
             string.Format("Sharing {0} originally from {1}", image.Title, image.MediaUrl);
            request.Data.SetDataProvider(StandardDataFormats.Bitmap, async dpr =>
            {
                var deferral = dpr.GetDeferral();

                var shareFile = await _settings.GetShareFileAsync(image.MediaUrl);
                var stream = await shareFile.OpenAsync(FileAccessMode.Read);
                dpr.SetData(RandomAccessStreamReference.CreateFromStream(stream));

                deferral.Complete();
            });
        }
    }
}
```

The beauty of sharing is that the Bing Image Search app can provide links and images without any knowledge of how consuming applications may use the information. While the Bing Image Search app is providing standard links and images, you could also envision providing more proprietary file type information and opening up the entire ecosystem of Windows apps that communicate with your apps, content, or files in ways you hadn't imagined.

The Bing Image Search app doesn't support being a share target. You will need to setup a declaration in your app manifest to display your Tile on the list, then your app will be activated with the entry point specified or into your `App.OnSharingTargetActivated` override as the default. For more information on handling Sharing as a target, see the samples online at *http://code.msdn.microsoft.com/windowsapps/Sharing-Content-Target-App-e2689782*.

Sensors

WinRT is meant to support modern hardware and sensors in a way Windows has never done in the past. One of those sensors that is of interest to the Bing Image Search app is the `Accelerometer`. The API for this sensor allows you to see when the user is physically shaking the device.

The events from the `Accelerometer` is different from other events like Search and Sharing because it happens so rapidly and subscribing to these events can, in some cases, actually turn on the physical hardware and ultimately drain the user's battery. Because of this, you want to be sparing in the use of the `Accelerometer`. In the case of the Bing Image Search app, I will be using this event only on the `SearchResultsPage` to load more images. Example 4-28 shows the registration and handling of the `Accelerometer` event.

Example 4-28. Accelerometer registration (SearchResultsPageViewModel.cs)

```
public class SearchResultsPageViewModel : BindableBase
{
    private readonly INavigationService _navigationService;
    private readonly IAccelerometer _accelerometer;

    public SearchResultsPageViewModel(INavigationService navigationService,
            IAccelerometer accelerometer /* other depedencies */)
    {
        _navigationService = navigationService;
        _accelerometer = accelerometer;

        _accelerometer.Shaken += accelerometer_Shaken;
        _navigationService.Navigating += NavigatingFrom;
    }

    private void NavigatingFrom(object sender, NavigatingCancelEventArgs e)
    {
        _accelerometer.Shaken -= accelerometer_Shaken;
        _navigationService.Navigating -= NavigatingFrom;
    }

    private void accelerometer_Shaken(object sender, object e)
    {
        LoadMore();
    }
}
```

The `SearchResultsPageViewModel` registers the `Accelerometer.Shaken` event when the ViewModel loads. Luckily, the ViewModel has an `AppBar` already set up for loading more images, so when the `Shaken` event occurs, I just call the same method for the `LoadMoreCommand`. The final piece of the `Accelerometer` is remembering to unsubscribe from the event when you no longer need it. To handle this, you'll notice an event called `NavigatingFrom`, which is fired whenever the `NavigationService` changes pages. I use this event to shut down the `Accelerometer`.

LockScreen

In addition to the high level native features that I've already discussed, Windows 8 has quite a few little features that apps may want to leverage. One of these features is the `LockScreen`. This screen displays a custom image for the user before they log in. On the `DetailsPageViewModel`, there is an `AppBar` button (Example 4-29 and Example 4-30). Similar to Set Tile and Save Image buttons, this button sends a `SetLockScreenMessage` to the message hub.

Example 4-29. Set Lock Screen AppBar Button (DetailsPage.xaml)

```
<Button x:Name="SetLockScreenCommand"Command="{Binding SetLockScreenCommand}"
        Style="{StaticResource SetLockScreenAppBarButtonStyle}" />
```

Example 4-30. SetLockScreen command (DetailsPageViewModel.cs)

```
public class DetailsPageViewModel
{
    // constructor and dependencies omitted
    public ICommand SetLockScreenCommand { get; set; }

    public async Task SetLockScreen()
    {
        await_messageHub.Send(new SetLockScreenMessage(_settings.SelectedImage));
    }
}
```

The message is handled by the `SetLockScreenHandler` (Example 4-31), which saves the image, updates the lock screen, and sets the status to display to the user. I'm using the `ApplicationSettings` to save the selected image as a new image in application storage called *LockScreen.jpg*. The reason I am storing it in application storage as a single name rather than using the actual name of the image, has to do with file storage. If I saved a unique image every time the user set the `LockScreen`, then I would have to clean up any other images and ensure I wasn't retaining unnecessary copies of files. By using the same name, when a user updates the lock screen to a new image, any old image is automatically overwritten. To make this handler testable I've also created a `LockScreenAdapter`, and as you can see in Example 4-32, it is very simple.

```csharp
public class SetLockScreenHandler : IAsyncHandler<SetLockScreenMessage>
{
    private readonly ApplicationSettings _settings;
    private readonly ILockScreen _lockScreen;
    private readonly IToastNotificationManager _toastNotification;

    public SetLockScreenHandler(ApplicationSettings settings, ILockScreen lockScreen,
        IStatusService statusService)
    {
        _settings = settings;
        _lockScreen = lockScreen;
        _statusService = statusService;
    }

    public async Task HandleAsync(SetLockScreenMessage message)
    {
        var file = await _settings.GetLockScreenFileAsync(message.Image.MediaUrl);
        await _lockScreen.SetImageFileAsync(file);

        _statusService.TemporaryMessage = string.Format("Image {0} set as lock screen.",
            message.Image.Title);
    }
}
```

Example 4-32. LockScreenAdapter (LockScreenAdapter.cs)

```csharp
public class LockScreenAdapter : ILockScreen
{
    public async Task SetImageFileAsync(IStorageFile file)
    {
        await LockScreen.SetImageFileAsync(file);
    }

    public async Task SetImageStreamAsync(IRandomAccessStream stream)
    {
        await LockScreen.SetImageStreamAsync(stream);
    }
}
```

Summary

Now that your app can take advantage of native features and participate in the new Windows 8 experience, you should get ready to start deploying your app. In the past, this meant creating installers, preparing deployment servers, and possibly creating CD-ROMs. Luckily this is not the case for Windows 8, and the Windows Store can help resolve the deployment issues from the past.

CHAPTER 5

Windows Store

The Windows Store is many things: it is an app that consumers use to install other apps onto their Windows 8 devices; it is an entity that maintains the quality of Windows applications for all users; and it can be a source of income for developers of all kinds. This chapter focuses on the information available to prepare your app so it can be deployed to the Windows Store.

 At the time of this writing, the Windows Store was not open to public submissions. If you visit some of the links that follow, you will receive a message stating, "We're sorry, but the Windows Store is currently closed to general registration. You need a registration code to register." At this time of this writing, registration codes are available only via a private invite system.

 Microsoft has a number of events where trained staff can review your app and potentially provide an invite. The event that I attended was available at *https://win8.msregistration.com*, but an Internet search for **win8 events** should get you started.

Marketing

As with personal relationships, first impressions are extremely important and if you are like me, you've been working on your app for many months and are excited to ship. However, your journey is not over, so set your expectations accordingly and plan for a few changes to your app. Also, once you read what is entailed in working through the Windows Store publication process, you may want to take a break from coding and focus on marketing without rushing to market.

Windows Store App

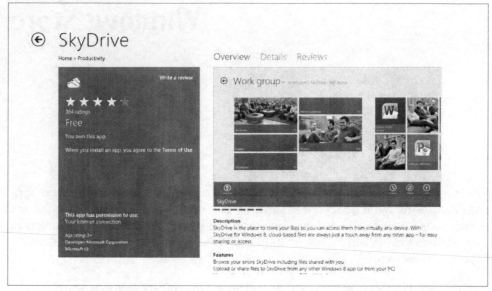

Figure 5-1. Windows Store App

The Windows Store App is the first place where a user will see your app. Figure 5-1 shows a screenshot of the Windows Store for the SkyDrive app. In order to publish your app to the Windows Store, you will need to prepare the content for this page. The following list contains the information that is needed for your app page:

Title or Name of your app
> The actual name of your application.

Tiles
> You will need to supply all the different-sized tiles used by your app. This should be easy because you've already created them for your app and specified them in your package manifest.

Screenshots
> Here you can provide anywhere between one and eight images of your application. A list of supported image sizes can be found at *http://msdn.microsoft.com/en-us/library/windows/apps/hh846296.aspx*. One of the easiest ways to create screenshots of your app is to use the simulator in Visual Studio. First, click the drop-down arrow beside the play button, and you will see a list of alternative debugging mechanisms. After selecting the simulator from this list, you will see a button for capturing a screenshot.

Category and subcategory
> Your app needs to specify a category and a subcategory from a list provided by the Windows Store.

Keywords

A list of keywords to help locate your app when consumers search for this type of app.

Description

A description of your app that is used to promote your app. Tips for writing a good description for you app can be found at *http://msdn.microsoft.com/en-us/library/windows/apps/hh694077*.

Countries

A list of the countries where your app will be available.

Release notes

A set of notes related to the latest release of your app or a running list of release notes for you app.

Release date

The date to release your app to the public, if not immediate.

Package

The actual code for the application, this contains the package manifest, which highlights the required capabilities of your app. The package is covered in more details later in this chapter.

More detailed information from Microsoft about the different required materials can be found online at *http://msdn.microsoft.com/en-us/library/windows/apps/hh694057*. Once you've prepared all the information that you need to deploy your app, you are ready to proceed.

Opening Your Developer Account

In order to publish your app to the Windows Store, you will need a developer account. To open your developer account, you can go to *http://go.microsoft.com/fwlink/?LinkId =220679* or in Visual Studio, select Project→Store→Open Developer Account. From here, you will be asked to sign in with a valid Windows Live ID.

 Opening your developer account requires a Windows Live ID. If you don't have one already, you are missing out on many features of Windows 8 that come from integrating your desktop with your Live ID. If you go to your user settings in the Windows 8 Control Panel, you can create one. You can also visit *http://www.live.com* and click the link on the left side under "Don't have a Windows Live ID?"

This is the account that will be associated with your app. If you would like your app to be published under a specific company account, you may choose to create a special account for this purpose, otherwise you can just use your personal Live ID. You will still be able to customize the name that will be displayed in the bottom-left corner of the app under *Developer*. After you've logged in, you will have to create your developer account, which will require a credit card and will give you access to create your app or just reserve your app name. Developer accounts are automatically renewed annually, depending on your time to market and your desire to proactively reserve your application name you may or may not want to purchase your account until you are ready to ship. Once you place your order, you start the clock on the billing process. If you are not ready to ship your app for more than six months, you'd be paying for unused time.

 Pricing plans are different for companies and personal accounts. A full list of pricing for the developer account can be found online at *http:// msdn.microsoft.com/en-US/library/windows/apps/hh694064*.

Upon logging in and creating your account, you will be taken to your app dashboard (Figure 5-2). From this screen, you can create a new app by clicking the link to submit an app on the left-side menu. You do not need to have your app packaged and ready to begin with this step, and you can save your progress at any point along the way.

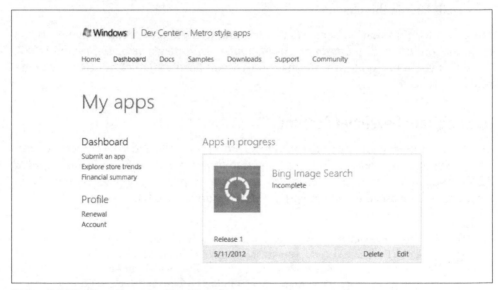

Figure 5-2. Windows Store App Dashboard

When you click Submit an App, you will be taken to the app submission page. This page is used as a workflow to guide you through the submission process. Microsoft has provided an estimated timeline as a guide so you know how long each step will take along the way (Figure 5-3). Even if you have not packaged and tested your app, you can begin to fill out the submission up to "Step 6: Packages."

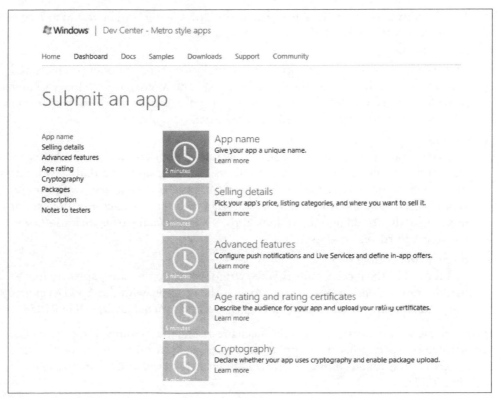

Figure 5-3. Windows Store App Submission Workflow

Selling Your App

There are many ways to monetize your app:

Collect the full price before download
> The traditional and most simple way to make money in an app store is to charge a price for your application before it can be downloaded. The Windows Store handles all aspects of the transactions on your behalf; there is no need for you to get involved in the individual transactions. There is a range of pricing tiers available starting at $1.49 and the Windows Store pays the industry standard 70% for every customer dollar. The Windows Store will provide batch payouts for all app purchases.

Time-limited or Feature-limited trial
> Any app can support a Try button on the Windows Store, which allows your app to be downloaded and used in a trial capacity. Options include limiting the time a consumer can use the app or limiting the features it supports. Some people may also choose a trial version of the app, which are full-featured version with ads; the user can then pay a flat rate to disable those ads at a later time if he so chooses.

More information about trial features in Windows 8 apps can be found at *http:// msdn.microsoft.com/en-US/library/windows/apps/hh694065*.

In-app purchases

The Windows Store also supports in-app purchases. Apps can offer products and features for purchase while the app is running. The Microsoft Developer Center provides details and best practices for in-app purchases at *http://msdn.microsoft .com/en-us/library/windows/apps/hh694067.aspx*.

Advertising

Apps can use ads to generate recurring revenue. If your app will retain the user's attention for long periods of time or if users visit your app on a daily basis, ads might offer more revenue than a single up-front purchase. Conversely, if your app is rarely used, you may not obtain enough ad impressions to make any money. For more info about adding ads to your apps, visit *http://advertising.microsoft.com/ windowsadvertising/developer*.

Third-party transactions

In addition to the mechanisms that the Windows Store provides, apps are free to handle transactions on their own as long as they comply with the App Developer Agreement at *http://msdn.microsoft.com/en-US/library/windows/apps/hh694058*.

If you choose to participate in one of the mechanisms that the Windows Store provides, you will need to specify this in the app submission page. More information about selling your apps can be found online at *http://msdn.microsoft.com/en-US/library/windows/ apps/br230836*.

Ratings and Reviews

The Windows Store automatically creates a rating system within every application. As with other platforms, the rating system in Windows 8 can and will be used for comments and bug reports if you don't provide a mechanism within your app to do so in a meaningful way. When focusing on the continued marketing of your app, it's imperative that you stay on top of the ratings and reviews and respond to them with updates if necessary. The guidance for Windows Phone and other mobile platforms serves as a great guide to managing the ratings system in the Windows Store. Alan Mendelevich at AdDuplex has a great series on Marketing and Monetizing your Windows Phone app and can be found online at *http://blog.adduplex.com*, which is a great resource for Windows 8 as well.

Distribution

At some point you'll be ready to ship your code. Visual Studio has made this process very simple by including everything you need to do in a Store menu that is available when you open a Windows 8 app project (Figure 5-4). There are a couple of features within the menu, but it serves three main purposes:

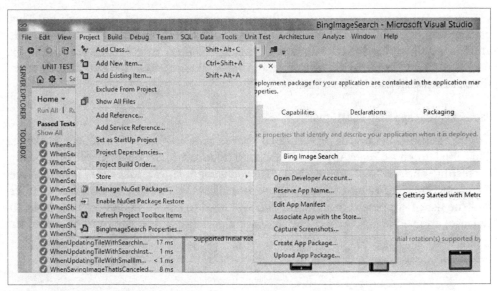

Figure 5-4. Visual Studio Store Options

Access to the Web Dashboard

From the dashboard you can see your existing apps, create new apps, edit your account info, and publish your app.

Preparing your app for deployment

You can upload screenshots or edit your application manifest to update capabilities, both of which are available through other mechanisms. There is also a custom application that will allow you to associate your app with the store so you can upload directly from Visual Studio.

Packaging your app for testing and deployment

The final piece creates your actual appx package. There is also a mechanism to upload your app directly to the Windows Store.

In addition to the items within the Visual Studio menu, you will also need to use the Windows App Cert Kit to verify your application. This app comes as part of the Windows SDK and can be found under `C:\Program Files\Windows Kits` or by typing `cert` on the start screen, but more on that later.

The first two steps in this distribution menu are ones that I covered earlier in the chapter; this next section focuses on the last step: packaging your app and testing for deployment.

Packaging Your App

Visual Studio can be used to deploy and test your app locally, on a remote machine, or on the local simulator. This process is great for testing, but cannot be used to distribute your app. When you are ready, you'll want to create an official appx package. This package can then be used to test locally, have your friends and other developers test, and eventually upload to the Windows Store. There are two ways to create your appx package, using Visual Studio or using the Appx Packager (`MakeAppx.exe`) directly from the command line.

Packaging your app from Visual Studio

In Visual Studio, with your project open choose Project→Store→Create App Package. This will launch a Create App Package wizard (Figure 5-5). If you are deploying locally for testing, choose "No" when asked, "*Do you want to build a package to upload to the Windows Store?*" The next screen (Figure 5-6) allows you to specify a version number and the list of supported processors. You will need to ensure that everything is set to Release, and then click Create. The final appx package will be deployed to the folder specified.

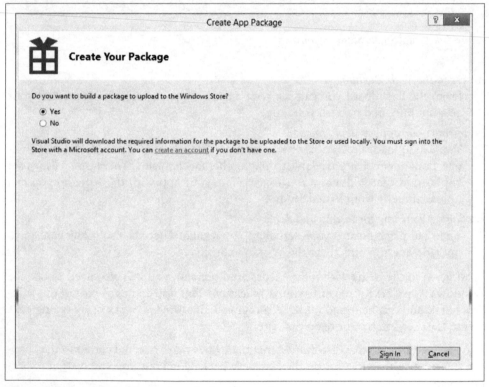

Figure 5-5. Visual Studio Create Appx Package Wizard

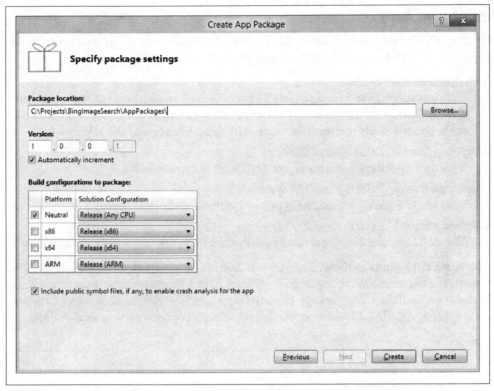

Figure 5-6. Visual Studio Create Appx Package Wizard (Page 2)

A full description of using Visual Studio for publishing your app can be found online at *http://msdn.microsoft.com/en-us/library/windows/apps/br230835.aspx*.

Packaging your app from the Appx Packager

Under the covers, the Visual Studio Wizard uses a command-line tool called the Appx Packager. This tool can be used directly via the command line or scripted as part of a continuous integration environment. Example 5-1 shows a rough example of what it would be like to create a similar appx package to what was created by the wizard in the previous section.

Example 5-1. Appx Packager command-line tool

```
MakeAppx.exe pack
    /d "C:\Projects\BingImageSearch\BingImageSearch\bin\Release\AppX"
    /p "C:\Projects\BingImageSearch\AppPackages\BingImageSearch_1.0.0.0_AnyCPU.appx"
```

Full details about the Appx Packager can be found online at *http://msdn.microsoft.com/en-us/library/windows/apps/hh446767.aspx*.

Inside your Appx

Once you've created your appx package you are ready to deploy. If you navigate to the deployment folder, you will see four files:

Add-AppxDevPackage.bat
> This is a script that is used to install your app. To install it you can right-click and choose Run as Administrator. This will launch a command line and execute PowerShell commands to install the code-signing certificate and the appx package.

BingImageSearch_1.0.0.0_AnyCPU.appx
> This appx package contains all the code for your application.

BingImageSearch_1.0.0.0_AnyCPU.appxsym
> This file is a package containing public symbols of the app package.

BingImageSearch_1.0.0.0_AnyCPU.cer
> The code signing certificate used to for protecting your appx from modification.

The appx package is nothing more than a ZIP file. To inspect its contents, you can rename the file extension to *.zip*. Figure 5-7 shows the folder with the extracted contents of the appx package. The package contains your assets, styles, images, xaml files, and code (in form of dlls). In addition, the appx package contains three generated files.

Assets	5/12/2012 3:15 PM	File folder
Common	5/12/2012 3:15 PM	File folder
[Content_Types].xml	5/12/2012 2:48 PM	XML Document
App.xaml	5/12/2012 2:48 PM	XAML File
AppxBlockMap.xml	5/12/2012 2:48 PM	XML Document
AppxManifest.xml	5/12/2012 2:48 PM	XML Document
AppxSignature.p7x	5/12/2012 2:48 PM	P7X File
BingImageSearch.exe	5/12/2012 2:48 PM	Application
DetailPage.xaml	5/12/2012 2:48 PM	XAML File
FileOpenPickerPage.xaml	5/12/2012 2:48 PM	XAML File
Metroloc.dll	5/12/2012 2:48 PM	Application extens...
NotificationsExtensions.dll	5/12/2012 2:48 PM	Application extens...
NotificationsExtensions.xml	5/12/2012 2:48 PM	XML Document
PreferencesPage.xaml	5/12/2012 2:48 PM	XAML File
resources.pri	5/12/2012 2:48 PM	PRI File
SearchHistoryPage.xaml	5/12/2012 2:48 PM	XAML File
SearchResultsPage.xaml	5/12/2012 2:48 PM	XAML File
Shell.xaml	5/12/2012 2:48 PM	XAML File

Figure 5-7. Appx Package Contents

[Content_Types].xml
> A standard openxml file for describing the contents of the package, specifically the block map and signature.

AppxBlockMap.xml
Contains a map of all files in the package and their respective hash values. These hash values can be validated just prior to launching to ensure that no files have been changed since the original appx package was created.

AppxSignature.p7x
The signature used to verify the AppxBlockMap.

Now that you've created your appx package, understood the contents, and installed it, you should be ready for the final stages of testing your app before deploying.

Running Windows App Cert Kit

The Windows App Cert Kit is a tool that is provided by Microsoft to help catch potential issues locally that could cause your app to fail certification. The tool mimics some of the tests that are performed by the certification team and tools within Microsoft. To launch the Windows App Cert Kit, type **cert** from the Start Screen.

When the Windows App Cert Kit loads (Figure 5-8), select Validate Windows 8 App. This will load a list of all the installed apps on your system. If you've installed your app, you should see it on the list. Be sure that no other applications are running, select your app, and click Next. This will launch your app multiple times and verify different performance metrics. As the message states, you should refrain from using your machine or interacting with the app during these tests. When the tests are complete, you will receive a list of test results.

Figure 5-8. Windows App Cert Kit

The Windows App Cert Kit checks the following things:

Eliminate Application Failures
> This is a simple test that fails if your app ever ceases to start throughout the testing process.

Windows 8 App Test Failure
> This verifies the schema and format of the app manifest. It also uses proprietary algorithms to ensure that your app does not try to access unprotected areas of the operating system or .NET.

Launch time performance
> Windows 8 apps are required to start within five seconds. If your app takes longer than that to start, it will not pass. You should look to delay loading of unnecessary resources or to implement some form of loading screen that will display a progress bar while your app is loading.

Suspend performance
> App suspension occurs frequently. In order to ensure good launch/suspend performance, apps should suspend within two seconds. In addition to time, apps will also need to keep CPU utilization below 50% and I/O usage less than 20MB to pass this test.

Test Appx Manifest Resources
> This test verifies that the files and settings configured in the app manifest are available and properly defined or sized.

Debug App Check
> This test checks whether your assemblies were built using the debug mode. This mode is not optimized for production and therefore, the Windows Store does not allow debug builds to be published publicly.

In addition to the items that are checked by the Windows App Cert Kit, you will also want to run through the Certification Requirements available at *http://msdn.microsoft .com/en-us/library/windows/apps/hh694083.aspx*. This list includes requirements with regard to design and layout of your application and also proper guidelines on rating your app for appropriate age groups. The next step will be publishing your app, so you'll want to be sure you've thoroughly tested your app and are confident that it is ready for submission to the Windows Store.

Publishing Your App

Publishing your app is actually very easy considering what you've already done to test your app locally. In order to create your app you will need to run the App Packager tool one more time, then navigate to the Windows Store Portal and upload your *.appx* or *.appxupload* file.

First you'll want to create your final deployment package now by following the steps from the "Packaging your app from Visual Studio" on page 84 section earlier. Inside

Visual Studio with your project open, navigate to Project→Store→Create App Package. This time you'll want to ensure you choose "Yes" when asked, *"Do you want to build a package to upload to the Windows Store?"*

With your final app package created, open the Windows Store Portal at *http://go.mi crosoft.com/fwlink/?LinkId=220679*. Assuming you've already started the process and entered your marketing and pricing information, you should be ready for Step 6: Packages. On the Packages screen (Figure 5-9), you will have the option to upload your app package. You can drag and drop it in or just click the link to locate your *.appx* or *.appxupload* file. Once you've completed this step, click Upload. Your package should now upload. The next two sections of this form are in regard to the description and notes to the testers. Once everything has completed you can submit your app.

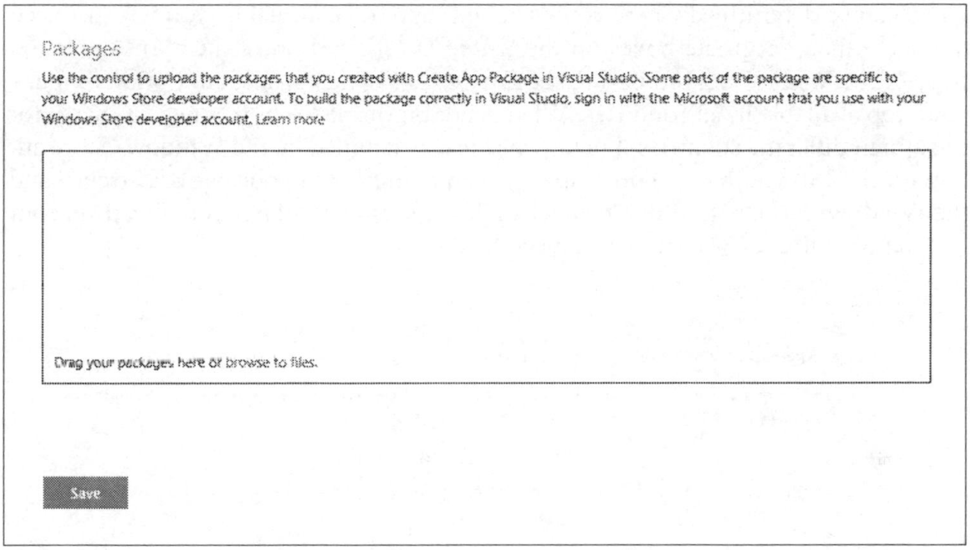

Figure 5-9. Upload Packages screen

The submission process may take a couple days. At this point, it's a waiting game, and I wish you luck. You should receive email notifications during the process, so be sure to check your junk mail folder just in case. You can also check back on the website for any updates.

Global Reach

As a developer, you've probably written apps numerous times for specific user communities. One of the powerful features of the Windows Store, and Windows in general, is that it's used throughout the world. This means that if you plan properly, you could reach an audience far beyond your initial expectations. If you choose to leverage this, you should take consideration of the nuances of different communities and languages.

This section focuses on two main areas of entering a global economy—exposure and localization.

Exposure to Global Markets

Regarding exposure to global markets, the Windows Store handles the majority of this burden for you. As a developer, you do not have to concern yourself with different currencies or different tax laws. The Windows Store will handle it. In order to take advantage of these features, there are two main decisions you will have to make:

1. Where do I want my app available?
2. What languages will my app will support?

Once you've determined where you want your app to be available, you will just need to check the appropriate boxes on the *Selling Details* section of the app submission page in the Windows Store portal, see Figure 5-10. There is also an option to make your app available in all countries. What is not on this list is how much to charge for the app in different countries. Luckily this, too, is handled by the Windows Store automatically. All you have to do is specify the pricing tier in your native currency and the Windows Store will automatically handle conversions and pay you directly in your own native currency without any concern.

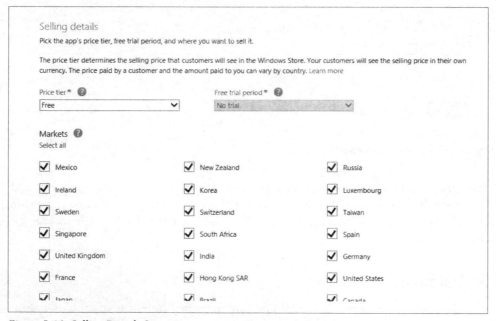

Figure 5-10. Selling Details Screen

The second question is considered *Localization* and impacts your code. In addition to changing your app, you will need to specify the appropriate countries in the *Selling Details* section so your localized app will be available in those specific markets.

Localization

Localization is a broad topic and the nuances of each different culture are far too vast to cover in this short guide. I will focus on setting up your app to support multiple languages and substituting text with translations. Your should try to set up all text output, from XAML or code, to be retrieved from a resource file early in the creation of your app. This is a good practice overall and allows for easy localization when the time comes.

Setting up resources

The first thing you'll need to do is provide localized resources. To do this, I created a new folder in the Assets folder called *en-us*. The name of this folder will be used to determine the proper language and culture that are supported by your application. Right-click on this folder and select New Item. When the dialog appears, choose Resource File (*.resw*). The name of this file doesn't matter and you can create as many Resource Files as you'd like to help organize your resources.

Localizing text in XAML

Now that you have your resource file set up, you can bind your XAML controls to the resource file directly. On one of your controls, you'll need to specify a unique id. The x:Uid property in Example 5-2 shows the button is set up with a unique id of "Home-Button". From here you will be able to specify any property you need for each specific language. In a simple case, you can create a new resource called "HomeButton.Content" where the ".Content" portion will tell the parser to set the resource text to the Content property on the button. Depending on your needs, you could also use this to specify a width for an element by providing a value in a resource with the key "Home-Button.Width". In the case of this example code, the Content would get overridden by the resource.

Example 5-2. Using Resources from XAML

```
<Button x:Uid="HomeButton" Content="Home" />
```

Localizing text in code

It's always been a best practice in .NET to use a resource file when specifying text to the user. Windows 8 apps are no exception. Using resources in Windows 8 apps is slightly different, but still simple. To access the resource you will need a new Resource Loader object. With this object, you can call GetString to return the localized version of any text (see Example 5-3).

Example 5-3. Using Resources in Code

```
var resources = new Windows.ApplicationModel.Resources.ResourceLoader();
var dialog = new MessageDialog(resources.GetString("Exception_NetworkUnavailable"));
await dialog.ShowAsync();
```

If you are interested in more information regarding localization, Tim Heuer has an excellent blog post on the topic available at *http://timheuer.com/blog/archive/2012/04/26/localize-windows-8-application.aspx*. You can also find information in the *Globalization preferences sample* on the Windows Dev Center.

 An important note from the comments of Tim Heuer's blog post is regarding a mysterious tag within the *package.appxmanifest*. This tag states `<Resource language="x-generate" />`. Tim points out that the Appx Packager will automatically generate the appropriate tags corresponding to the appropriate folder names within your solution. If you override this value, you will be responsible for manually configuring this tag with every deployment.

Summary

Application development is always a journey. Hopefully this book has helped you get started on the process of building your application. The story regarding Windows 8 and information on developing applications will only get better as time progresses. Whether you are part of a team or a solo developer, I hope the development experience and the benefits of the Windows ecosystem are as helpful and advantageous to you as they are to me.

About the Author

Ben Dewey is employed at Tallan as a Senior Software Developer where he consults on many projects around New York City, focusing on Architecture, Silverlight, ASP.NET, and jQuery. He also works to develop Server Oriented Applications using WCF. Ben strives to create SOLID applications of the highest craftsmanship while paying special attention to clean User Experiences (UX). Ben is currently a committer on the Apache Stonehenge project, and is actively involved in numerous community events, from speaking at local user groups and helping to organize the ALT.NET Meetup in NYC.

Have it your way.

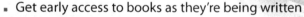

Lightning Source UK Ltd
Milton Keynes UK
UKOW020749051012

200083UK00002B/10/P